MAKE CHRISTIANITY GREAT AGAIN

P. ANDREW SANDLIN

ALSO BY P. ANDREW SANDLIN

The Full Gospel: A Biblical Vocabulary of Salvation

Keeping Our Sacred Trust: Biblical Authority, Creedal Orthodoxy, and Heresy
(editor)

New Flesh, New Earth: The Life-Changing Power of the Resurrection

Backbone of the Bible: Covenant in Contemporary Perspective
(editor)

Un-Inventing the Church: Toward a Modest Ecclesiology

The Birthday of the King: A Christmas Book

Dead Orthodoxy or Living Heresy?

Wrongly Dividing the Word: Overcoming the Law-Gospel Distinction

Christian Culture: An Introduction

The Christian Sexual Worldview

Holy Week for an Unholy World

God Was in Christ Reconciling

God Decides What Is Normal

Many of these works are available digitally at Amazon.com.

Copyright © 2019 by P. Andrew Sandlin

All rights reserved.

No part of this book may be reproduced in any form or by any electronic or mechanical means, including information storage and retrieval systems, without written permission from the author, except for the use of brief quotations in a book review.

❦ Created with Vellum

To Pastor Dr. Ron and Mrs. Linda Smith, God's choice servants, and my dear friends

Our Lord and King will never negotiate a truce with his enemy. Nor will he retreat from the battle field. He maintains his forces against his opponents, and never waivers. That's how it was when you and I were children. So it remains now that we are adults, and it continues into our old age. When we die and depart to the greener pastures, the battle will continue over our graves, and there will be no end until he, who will open all graves, returns.

— ABRAHAM KUYPER

CONTENTS

Preface	xi
1. The Christian Assault on Christendom	1
2. First, the Kingdom	10
3. Stand Your Ground in the Evil Day	14
4. Resistance Theology Versus resignation Theology	18
5. A Curse on Aborticide	22
6. Biblical Sexuality, Simply Explained	26
7. Three Axioms on Homosexuality in the Church	31
8. Reforming Only the Family and Church Won't Suffice	33
9. Liberal Christianity Isn't	37
10. Armed to the Teeth, Pacifist to the Core	41
11. Creation: The Evangelical Failure	45
12. The Revenge of the Cosmos	48
13. The Thinness of the Church	52
14. The Progressives' March Toward God's Judgment	56
15. A Note on Faith, Works, and Justification	61
16. Christmas versus Excarnation	63
17. Our Romantic Moment	67
18. The Romantic Cult of Authenticity	71
19. Letters on the Current Protestant Revival of Classicism, Scholasticism, and Natural Theology	74
20. Covenant versus Autonomy	77
21. Saccharine Piety	80
Notes	85
About the Author	91
About the Center for Cultural Leadership	93

PREFACE

This book constitutes a collection of short essays on an array of topics. Many first appeared at my blog, docsandlin.com. Others were excerpted from lectures or sermons I've delivered over the past three or four years.

The title is a variation on President Donald Trump's successful campaign slogan, Make America Great Again (MAGA). As a slogan, it is perfectly sensible. America was once great, but its greatness has diminished. Making America great again is a worthy objective. But we won't know how to do that if we don't know what made America great in the first place.

Similarly, Christianity's greatness has diminished. I refer to Christianity historically and culturally considered in the West. By contrast, the greatness of the Christian Faith objectively understood has not lessened: the Lord Jesus Christ and his word and the Cross and resurrection, for example, are just as great today as they ever were. But the Faith at is practiced in the West and particularly as it influences what we nowadays call "public" life is at a low ebb. This diminution has occurred before historically both in the West as well as in the rest of the world, and it has been recovered.

PREFACE

A contribution toward that recovery in our own time is the chief objective of this small book.

THE CHRISTIAN ASSAULT ON CHRISTENDOM

*C*hristians are quick to blame secularists and neo-pagans for the cultural marginalization of our Faith, but much of it is due to our own timidity, compromise, and cowardice. Before he ascended, our Lord charged the first Christians to disciple the nations (Mt. 28:18–20). It was a bold charge that demands a bold life and message. At the first post-resurrection Pentecost, a radically reenergized Peter, transformed from a craven Christ-denier to a fierce Christ-proclaimer (Ac. 2), declared to thousands of Jews: "[K]now assuredly that God has made this Jesus, whom you crucified, both Lord and Christ" (v. 36). This is the basic message of the New Testament and the primitive church, and it is the first Christian creed: Jesus is Lord.[1]

This message has impelled Christians whenever the Faith has advanced in the world. Despite relentless persecution, the primitive church marched boldly in that message. Finally, even the Roman emperor Constantine had to bow before Jesus Christ. Gradually Christian culture pervaded the West. In fact, Western civilization became roughly synonymous with Christian civilization. The Reformation sought to correct severe theological abuses in the medieval church, but it did not oppose Christian culture. Far from it.

P. ANDREW SANDLIN

Its English-speaking heirs, the Puritans, believed that all society should be governed by God's law in the Bible. England's American colonies each had established churches or Christian establishment of some kind, as did every one of the first United States.[2]

THE LOST CHRISTENDOM

Nobody reading these lines has ever seen Christendom. Christendom began with Constantine's public affirmation of Christianity in the 4th century; engulfed both Eastern and, later, Western Europe; and then shaped the European colonies in the New World. It was Byzantine and Roman Catholic and (later) Protestant.

Christendom died incrementally, first in Western Europe by the mid-18th century under the pressures of the Enlightenment and its subsequent reaction, Romanticism. In the United States after the Civil War, Christendom was shredded by Darwinism, higher Biblical criticism, and secular democracy. Christendom in the East was always subservient to the state, and when the state became atheistic (Marxist) in Russia in 1917 and in Eastern Europe in 1945–1946, Christendom simply collapsed.

FADED GLORY

The Greatness Christianity of former days is now in retreat everywhere. The 18th century European Enlightenment ripped away the miraculous. Romanticism eroded all objective Christian standards, like the Bible. Darwinism reduced man to an amoral higher animal. More recently, postmodernism depicts man as an inventor of himself and of his own conceptual and moral universe. Christianity is now largely confined to isolated family life and to Sunday church. Christian schools and colleges dot the landscape, but many are caving in to the spirit of the age, particularly same-sex-"marriage." Everywhere the Lord's Day is dishonored. A robust, full-bodied Faith is in full-scale power-down mode.

What was Christendom? It was the visible, public affirmation of

Christianity by nations and cultures. It was Christian civilization marked out by Trinitarian baptism, profession of the ecumenical Christian creeds, and allegiance to the Bible and to the Faith once for all delivered to the saints (Jude 3). Christendom was a ubiquitous, transnational way of life shaped by the Bible and Christian tradition. National political leaders weren't just Christians in their private lives — they were expected to apply their expression of Christianity (however warped and imperfect) in the state. Likewise, law, music, education, literature, science, technology, poetry — all aspects of life were expected to pay tribute to Jesus and Savior and Lord. Society was to be a Christian culture.

Christendom wasn't perfect — far from it — but it was a concrete historic reality.[3]

THE EARLY ENEMIES

Christendom has always had enemies — from outside it was assaulted by Islam. Even fringe sectors of Christians like the Anabaptists decried it. But Christendom's biggest enemy became the Enlightenment. Make no mistake: some early Enlightenment figures like John Locke and Thomas Jefferson were not Christian but were Christian-influenced, yet over time, the chief tenet of Enlightenment[4] — that no authority could sit in judgment on human reason, that man's reason and experience were the measure of all things — suffocated Christendom. The earliest and most violent public exhibition of this suffocation was the French Revolution, which swept away a corrupt and tyrannical state along with a corrupt and effete church. What replaced a corrupt church and state was infinitely worse than its predecessors — as the Parisian guillotine could attest. The French Revolution was the mother of all violent secular revolutions — in Russia, China, Korea, Cambodia and Vietnam. Wherever those secular revolutions prevailed, Christendom vanished.

In established liberal democracies like England and the United States, the revolution was not violent, but it was no less successful. Secularization won out by gradually (democratically, culturally, subtly, peacefully) capturing the public schools and universities, the major foundations, the arts, and politics.[5] This means of cultural takeover was no less effective than violent revolution — just as Hitler's democratic election in the Weimer Republic installed him no less securely than a revolution would have.

Today Christendom is a distant memory — or no memory at all. Secularism is an "invisible ideology"; it's a way of life almost nobody questions and almost everybody takes for granted. This aversion to or ignorance of Christendom is understandable — secularists want a secular world, not a Christian world — and they've got one.

CHRISTIANS AND CHRISTENDOM

What's harder to understand is the *Christian* assault on Christendom. After all, wouldn't you think that Christians would want the Gospel to change the world and for Jesus to be Lord of all things everywhere? Yes, you'd think so. But you'd be wrong. Large sectors of contemporary Christianity deplore Christendom — they think the church took a disastrous turn with Constantine and that in many ways secularism has saved the church from Christianity's long-time civilizational dominance.

If that idea sounds perverse, it's because it is. Here are two recent examples of this perversity.

BRIAN MCLAREN'S EMERGENT MASOCHISM

Brian McLaren, noted pastor and godfather of the Emergent Movement, rightly intertwines Christendom and Western civilization — and laments both. He deplores "Western Christianity's dark side," by which he means its colonialism, market economics, "white privilege," institutional racism, militarism, and so on.[6] This is common liberal and secularist drivel. Of course, Christendom was far from perfect (lamentably there were [for example] racists in Christendom, just as there were — and are — racists among secularists). But, by and large, Christendom brought to the West (over time) political liberty, individual rights, economic prosperity, protection for minorities, and artistic excellence. To secularists who scoff at this assertion ("Wasn't Christendom rife with religious persecution, political tyranny, poverty, and retrogressive culture, until secularism liberated the world?") the answer is simply, No. These tragedies did at times exist in Christendom — *and it was in Christendom in which they were mostly abolished.* Christendom doesn't eliminate sin, but it does have recourse to the sources that mitigate sin — namely God and his Word.

Brian McLaren's hatred (the word is not excessive) for Christendom seems a form of spiritual masochism. He wants a weak, marginal faith.[7] He rightly knows that Paul said that God's strength was perfected in Paul's personal weakness (2 Cor. 12:9), but McLaren seems to miss the King of kings and Lord of lords who rules the world in might, judging his enemies (Rev. 11–21) and vesting his saints with godly, humble dominion and stewardship of the world (Eph. 1:15–23; Rev. 2:26; 3:21; Dan. 7:18–27). Brian opts for weak-kneed Christianity, which he equates with real Christianity. Christendom isn't compatible with weak-kneed Christianity, so Brian simply jettisons it.

DAVID VANDRUNEN'S REFORMED ANTI-CHRISTENDOM

A second example of aversion to Christendom is David VanDrunen, professor at Westminster Seminary California, an avowedly Reformed institution. The historically alert reader may be scratching his head. Has any sector of the church (aside from Roman Catholicism) so stressed Christendom than Reformed Christianity? Wasn't Calvin committed to a distinctly Christian Geneva? And did not Zwingli and Bucer and Bullinger and Knox affirm Christendom? They did. But Dr. VanDrunen isn't happy with this.[8] Christian culture is the visible exhibition of Christendom, but David opposes Christian culture, or, rather, radically redefines it as the church.[9] VanDrunen wants a churchly Christianity and no distinctive Christianity outside the church. He mildly criticizes Calvin, who "was living in the midst of Christendom"[10] mistakenly assimilating Christendom at times. But

VanDrunen's bigger targets are Abraham Kuyper and the "Neo-Calvinists."[11]

Kuyper, a towering figure in Reformed history,[12] was a pastor, theologian, university president and for a time even prime minister of the Netherlands. He was an unflagging advocate of Christian culture and, therefore, of Christendom. His heirs (the "Neo-Calvinists") are even worse, according to VanDrunen, for wanting to redeem all of culture and subordinate it to Christ the King, Christianizing *everything*. This is the Christian cultural mandate, God's original commission to Adam and Eve to steward the earthy for his glory (Gen. 1:28–30), taking humble dominion in the earth, though this commission has now (since the Fall) been adapted to account for sin and redemption. VanDrunen holds that this program is wrong on three counts.

First, it devalues the church, since the Neo-Calvinists believe the kingdom is bigger than the church. If the kingdom is bigger than the church, then Christendom is a distinct possibility.

Second, Neo-Calvinism swerves from the New Testament, which is mostly about the transitory nature of life, heavenly citizenship and suffering, not about Christianizing culture.

Third, Christians shouldn't take earthly stewardship or exert godly dominion as Adam was commanded to do since Jesus, as the Second Adam, has already done that for them.

MEETING OBJECTIONS

What do we say to these objections? They are wrong.

First, the kingdom is bigger than the church. Jesus preached about the kingdom all the time (Mt. 3:2; 4:17; 6:10; 18:3; 19:14; 21:43; 25:1, 14, 34; 26:29) and only rarely talked about the church, at least in his utterances recorded in the Bible (Mt. 16:18; 18:17). Of course, Jesus didn't have to use the word "church" to refer to it, but nobody reading the Gospels would get the impression that the church is identical to the kingdom. The kingdom is God's reign in the earth now centered in the Messiah (1 Cor. 15:24–28). The church is his body of believers in the earth (Eph. 1:22–23, 5:22–32). The church is a critical aspect of the kingdom. Both church and kingdom are vital; but the kingdom is bigger than the church (more about this in the next chapter).

Second, the New Testament talks plenty about the transitory nature of life, heavenly citizenship and suffering, but these aren't its only life orientation, and, after all, the Bible, not just the New Testament, is our source of authority. Jesus assures his disciples that the obedient will be blessed *in this life* (Mk. 10:30); he calls his followers to disciple all nations, not just individuals (Mt. 28:18–20); and he promises that all those united to Jesus are heirs of the entire world, not just heaven (Rom. 4:13). The New Testament promises temporality, heavenly citizenship and suffering, *as well as* godly dominion, blessings, and Gospel success.

Third, Jesus did indeed take dominion, but his faithful followers join him in his dominion task (Rom. 16:20; Rev. 2:26; 3:21). Jesus' obedience in taking dominion as the Second Adam was not in order that we need *not* obey in assuming Adam's task. Jesus' initiatory, redemptive obedience makes our responsive, non-redemptive obedience possible (Rom. 5:12–6:1–23).

David writes that God never designed Christianity to build civilizations,[13] but he hasn't offered a persuasive Biblical case for this view, and he has implicitly verified that he is breaking with significant elements of his own tradition in assaulting Christian civilization.

REBUILDING CHRISTENDOM

If Christians are charged with stewarding the world for God's glory; if we are commissioned to disciple all nations; if Jesus is Lord of all things, not just the family and church — then rebuilding Christendom must be an objective of Christianity. I said "rebuilding Christendom," not *resurrecting* Christendom. Constantinian and medieval and Reformation Christendom had their day and made their contribution. What we must be after today is a new Christendom built on the best aspects of the past but open to new ideas and practices in line with the Bible.

But it's premature to start rebuilding Christendom full-tilt as long as the vast majority of Christians are assaulting or oblivious to it. As badly as we need a revival of fervent prayer and holiness, godly parenting in the family, a church drenched in devotion to Jesus Christ and powerful preaching and communion, and the Christianization of art, education, politics, science, law and so on — we need as much for Christians to radically reorient themselves to the Lordship of Jesus Christ and his comprehensive claims on us that require Christendom.

RESTORATION OF GREATNESS

Christians are required to be humble about themselves, but never about their God. If we boast, we must boast in the Lord (2 Cor. 10:17). Our Lord is a great God. He is the cosmic sovereign (Eph. 1:20–23). He rules the universe. His gospel brings sinners to repentance and saves them by his matchless grace. If there is to be a restoration of Christianity's greatness, there must be a retrieval of these convictions that made Christianity great in the first place. The first apostles spoke the word of God with boldness. They were witnesses of our Lord's resurrection. They heard with their own ears the Great Commission. They knew the Lord promised that hell's very gates would not prevail when the church came attacking (Mt. 16:18).

The claims of King Jesus are not options. He commands all men everywhere to repent (Ac. 17:30) and this means to trust him for salvation, and bow to his authority. The entire world is subject to God's law (Rom. 3:20). The Great Commission is to disciple the nations with the glorious, love-drenched, obligatory gospel. This gospel transforms lives and cultures. To say the gospel transforms lives but not cultures flies in the face not only of abundant historical testimony but also, and more importantly, the Bible itself. In whatever Christians do, they are to do for God's glory (1 Cor. 10:31). Jesus came to subordinate *all* enemies, not just non-cultural enemies (1 Cor. 15:20–27). This command extends far beyond church and private devotions.

CONCLUSION

Whenever the church has marched with this message, she has gained ground. She has routed the forces of Satan, death, and hell, and gradually produced a Christian culture. Christianity gave us the dignity of the human person, the university, political liberty, modern science and medicine, a purified sexuality, the exultation of women, transcendent music, and the abolition of slavery.[14] These were not bequeathed to Western civilization by the Greco-Roman world, ancient paganism, Islam, or secularism. They're the fruits of Christianity. The West has come to take these fruits for granted, and assumed it can uproot the tree and still get the fruit. This is a dangerous illusion. As our civilization turns from God, it will gradually lose the great blessings that have made it what it is.

Meanwhile, Christians must recover their triumphant boldness, proclaiming the slain Lamb who is the Lion, ruling from the heavens. We must not gently suggest that Jesus is the best way. We must trumpet that he is the only way, and all other ways lead to individual, cultural, and eternal destruction. True greatness is found only in our great king of Kings and Lord of lords. To lose him is eventually to lose everything, everywhere. To have him is eventually to have everything, everywhere.

When Christians return to the idea of Christendom as an *operating assumption* and not merely a pleasant historic artifact or even an objective, we'll be on our way to a restored godly world.

FIRST, THE KINGDOM

When Jesus cautioned his disciples not to be anxious over earthly provision but to seek first God's kingdom, since the Father supplies their every need (Mt. 6:24–34), he was laying out God's priority for his followers' overarching life commitment. Loving God in the totality of our being is the first great *commandment* (Mk. 12:28–32). The cultural mandate is the first great *commission* (Gen. 1:27–30). But the kingdom of God is the first great *commitment*. The kingdom of God is the reign of God.[1]

The Psalmist highlighted that universal reign (Ps. 2, 45, 72, 110, *e.g.*). Jesus came preaching it (Mt. 4:12–17). It begins in the heart of the Christian and works its way outward to all of life and society (Lk. 17:20–21; 1:33). The kingdom reveals God's objective as his life-giving, joy-inspiring, world-flourishing rule in the cosmos. As the cosmos' Creator, God knows what's best for it, what delights and benefits man, what brings both him and man himself consummate glory. To willingly submit to Jesus Christ as Lord according to the Father's command by the Spirit's power is to live life to the fullest, life as God intended from Eden. The gospel is therefore truly the *good news of the kingdom* (Lk. 8:1). The good news is that in Jesus Christ, God is overcoming the bad news of sin, corruption, and condemnation. Just as the bad news is not limited to the individual heart and destiny, so the good news is not limited to the individual heart and destiny. The curse afflicts all creation. But the gospel goes "far as the curse is found." That means everywhere.

SATAN'S RIVAL KINGDOM

It should come as no surprise that Satan, whose desire to unseat God incited his downfall, spearheads a rival kingdom (Mt. 12:26). "Fall down and worship me," he implored our Lord in the wilderness temptation (Mt. 4:8–9). Lucifer fell because he attempted to overthrow God Almighty (Is. 14:12–15). He is called "the god of this world" (2 Cor. 4:4), that is, the god of the world *system* committed to contesting God's kingdom. History since Genesis 3 constitutes the cosmic war between rival kingdoms — God's and Satan's. Satan is not simply trying to seduce sinners to eternal damnation; he is also angling to control and enslave the present world. He will not succeed, but he will fight with increasing fury, knowing his cause is doomed (Rev. 12:12).

It is because victory in this cosmic war is God's plan for history that Jesus stated that his disciples are to seek his kingdom first. The kingdom is not a means to an end. It *is* the end, both as God's objective, and in the historical sequence (1 Cor. 15:20–28). All else contributes to this end.

THE CHURCH IS NOT THE KINGDOM

The church, for example, is a vital aspect of, but not identical to, the kingdom. The church is Christ's body (Col. 1:18), for whom God's very blood in his Son was shed (Ac. 20:28). To minimize the church is to minimize a sizable component of the kingdom. But the kingdom is wider than the church. I once heard a church leader say, "The church is God's Plan A, and there is no Plan B." It is more correct to say, "The kingdom is God's Plan A, and the family and church and state are Plans 1A, 2A, and 3A." The kingdom is The Plan. Everything else contributes to that plan. Make no mistake: To dismiss or marginalize the church is to dismiss or marginalize Christ's body and bride. Today Christians somehow think they can bypass the church and still please God. No Christian in biblical (or patristic, or later) times would (or could) have dreamed of such a thing. The church is vital to the kingdom of God.

But the church is *not* the kingdom of God, and collapsing the kingdom into the church is dangerously limiting the rule of God. God is as interested in governing and ruling the culture outside the church as he is the church itself. Today in understandable reaction to the anti-church sentiment, many Christians seem to believe that our entire religious efforts should be expended on the church. Neo-orthodox theologian Karl Barth went so far as to say, "Theology is . . . a function in the liturgy of the church."[2] It is hard to imagine a more culturally irrelevant view of theology. Theology can no more be limited to the church or liturgy than the Bible can. Barth and evangelicals who follow his view today practice what Joseph Boot terms Churchianity.[3] They ecclesiasticize the Faith and the kingdom. They care little for God's authority in education, politics, music, science, technology, entertainment — in the culture outside the church. The church should not simply be training "full-time" church workers but encouraging Christians to develop a distinctively Christian worldview and apply it in the field to which God has called them in their 9-to-5 vocation. The goal of the kingdom is to capture and reorient every area of culture presently under the reign of sin, that is, Satan's kingdom. This task is obviously much larger than the church. It will perhaps come as a surprise that the Protestant reformer John Calvin saw the calling of the civil magistrate, what we today term a politician, as an even higher calling than a pastor (Calvin himself was a pastor.)[4] He might have been wrong in this assessment (I believe he was), but at least he understood that the kingdom of God could never find its zenith in the church.

CONCLUSION

We followers of King Jesus are to seek first his kingdom. Aspects of the kingdom, like church, family, the state, vocation, business, our personal welfare and future, must contribute to that kingdom, to that *rule* in the earth. We are not to be self-centered, church-centered, family-centered, or politics-centered. We are to be kingdom-centered. This is identical to saying that are to be God-centered. When we stand one day before the King, the urgent question confronting us will be: have we, as our life's mission, pressed the King's work, his kingdom, in our lives?

STAND YOUR GROUND IN THE EVIL DAY

BLUE-JEANS RELIGION

Christian leaders who until the last five years stood for biblical truth and historic orthodoxy are caving in record numbers to what Francis Schaeffer called "forms of the world spirit":[1] Cultural Marxism ("social justice"),[2] "wokeness," ideological feminism, same-sex "marriage" and "-attraction," "Christian socialism," and upgraded Darwinism. These "thought leaders" among evangelicals, the Southern Baptist Convention, the Presbyterian Church in America, the Gospel Coalition, and numerous churches and other ministries decry "toxic masculinity," "white privilege," and the literal historical account of Genesis. Faithful followers, accustomed to trusting their leaders, are unsettled and perplexed. Has the church in the West really been guilty of "systemic racism"? Must Christians accept same-sex lust as normative? Are males simply presumed to be guilty of misusing power with females? Is insisting on the historicity of Adam and Eve a barrier to the Gospel? It's no wonder so many in the pews are anxious.

While Christian leaders can be sincere but misled, there can be little doubt that the chief impetus behind the current wholesale defection is simply craven compromise, the desire to curry favor and popularity in an apostate age suckled on individual autonomy. When leaders change their views on historically (and biblically) settled issues just a few years after these issues have become unsettled (and re-settled as apostasy) in the wider culture, we can be confident that we're observing compromise, not sincere 6.rethinking. A shift would be more laudable if it cut *against* the grain of the cultural fabric: if, for example, a Christian college president concluded that his institution should issue a formal declaration repudiating Obamacare, or that after much prayer a pastor proposes the church amend its statement of faith to expressly oppose both garden-variety KKK racism as well as Left-wing "affirmative action" racism.[3] It takes no courage, Francis Schaeffer taught us in the late 60's, to wear blue jeans as an anti-establishment statement when almost everybody is wearing blue jeans.[4]

DON'T FOLLOW ERRANT LEADERS

Meanwhile, followers, church members, laypersons, and patrons would be well advised to heed these items of counsel. First, the fact that your leaders change doesn't mean you must change. The Bible is replete with warnings to errant leaders of godly followers, issued from the old covenant prophets to John the apostle. The calling of leaders is precarious precisely because of their measure of influence (Jas. 3:1). But sheep are not required to follow errant shepherds, and certainly not wolves. Don't simply assume a pastor or popular speaker is faithful to the Lord. Don't suppose that the size of his audience (or number of Twitter followers) is the measure of his faithfulness. Examine his (or her!) teaching in light of the Scriptures. If the apostle Paul commended his followers for scrutinizing his own teaching (Ac. 17:10–11), you can be certain that he expected all Christian followers to follow their lead.

DON'T BE SENTIMENTAL ABOUT INSTITUTIONS

Second, don't be sentimental about institutions. If they leave the Faith, you must leave them. Churches that were once faithful to the Lord have drifted toward heresy (like City Church-San Francisco). Christian ministries that once championed Biblical faith have become little more than social clubs (the Salvation Army is a striking example). Christian colleges and seminaries that began with godly men on their knees wishing to establish a training center for devout young Christians have been gradually infested by unbelief, higher criticism, socialism, Darwinism, and Cultural Marxism. This is true of every Ivy League college, and increasingly true of a number of evangelical colleges and seminaries (like Wheaton and Azusa Pacific). Christians associated with these sorts of churches and institutions sometimes feel a sentimental loyalty: "I've been attending here for 40 years, and I feel comfortable." Or, "My parents are buried in the church cemetery." Or, "I'm a graduate of this college or seminary and just can't pull away." And they allow their sentimentality to blind them to the apostasy before their eyes. Many continue to support this apostasy with their attendance and money. This is wrong.[5] Abandon apostasy and redirect your prayer, time, effort, and money toward orthodox, Bible-believing, uncompromising, culture-reclaiming churches and ministries. The fact that sectarians draw the lines too quickly and narrowly (over denominational distinctives, for example) doesn't mean there are no lines. There are bold, God-drawn lines, and they must not be crossed.

DON'T STAY MUTE IN THE FACE OF EVIL

In Ephesians 5:11 Paul writes, "Take no part in the unfruitful works of darkness, but instead expose them." We don't have the luxury of obeying only the first half of that verse.[6] The second half of that verse puts pressure on today's craven Christianity, which says, "I know that I must avoid sin, and I'll obey in order to please God. But other people have to make up their own minds. They're responsible for their own actions. That's their business, not mine. I'll just go about my own life." But that is precisely what Paul does not say. He commands, first, that we separate ourselves entirely from the works of darkness. He also commands that we expose those works. In other words, it's not sufficient quietly and covertly to avoid evil. We must overtly expose it. The prime reason that we today find this expectation distasteful is that we have a diminished view of God's holiness. God deplores sin. It diminishes; it deranges, it destroys, and it damns. Curbing sin is a God-honoring act. We must, of course, curb it first in our own lives, and only then in the lives of others, always charitably; and we must never limit that exposure to the "private" sphere. We must expose cultural evils no less than individual evils. The Bible places a high premium on unity, and we dare not sunder it for "light and transient causes." But Cultural Marxism, homosexuality, and socialism are not light and transient causes.

CONCLUSION

Ours is an age of rampant social depravity but, in addition, and even more tragically, pervasive defection within the church. It is analogous to what happened about 100 years ago when Protestant liberalism captured almost all of the mainline denominations in the U.S. and England. We will win the war, but there will be no victory without battles. We must stand charitably, firmly, without rancor, but also without flinching. Remember at all times that our great enemy is Satan and his minions. Soon in eternity we must stand before the Lord. Until then our charge is: Stand your ground in the evil day (Eph. 6:13).

RESISTANCE THEOLOGY VERSUS RESIGNATION THEOLOGY

One day a worm that had been burrowing into the forehead of a medieval Mother Superior fell out as she bent over. Believing that all human suffering is God's will, she reinserted the worm into her forehead.[1] She was committed to the pervasive, masochistic, and evil theology of *resignation* rather than *resistance*: Christians should resign themselves to the triumph of evil since it suits God's covert, inscrutable, but ultimately good purposes.

A theology of resistance, by radical contrast, knows that God doesn't rule the world arbitrarily, maintaining a covert plan conflicting with his revealed plan in the Bible. Evil, which began with Satan's cosmic insurrection and invaded earth in the Garden of Eden, constitutes war on God's purposes. While God is so powerful that he can use even evil to fulfill those purposes (Ps. 76:10), he abominates evil; and he sent his Son to die on the Cross and rise from the dead to crush it (1 Jn. 3:8). The Gospel, in fact, is God's evil-crushing program.[2] The existence of evil anywhere is an affront to a holy God, and, though he is longsuffering, he will not perpetually abide it.

RESIGNATION THEOLOGY

A nefarious weapon in Satan's arsenal is convincing God's people that his secret purposes somehow include the victory of evil. The logic is generally this: God alone knows what's best, and sometimes the victory of evil is best, so he secretly decrees its victory, and we dare not resist it. The Bible never actually says this, of course, or even teaches it; but it often serves people who desire a rationale for passivity or weariness (or, less excusably, laziness or cowardice) in the face of ubiquitous evil. This rationale is fashioned into a theology: the theology of resignation. Resignation theologians invoke exceptional episodes in the Bible, like God's revelation to Jeremiah to warn the apostate Jews not to oppose the impending Babylonian invasion since captivity was his righteous punishment for their sin (Jer. 27, 28). It's vital to recall, however, that this resignation was divinely revealed; it was not a speculation about God's alleged secret purposes (so common among Christians today). In almost every case, God's *revealed* purpose (never different from his secret purpose) is for his people to resist evil. The superficial piety of resignation theology appeals to sincere but naïve Christians: "More than anything, I wish to submit to the will of God, even if it means evil triumphs." But the triumph of evil is never the will of God. Even evil in the form of punishment on the wicked or God's people (like Babylon with Israel) is an intermediate step toward the judgment of evil itself: God promised Israel that after he used Babylon for his purposes of judgment, he would brutally cast them aside and restore his people (Jer. 24:12–14). Apart from verbal divine revelation declaring otherwise, God's will is always to resist evil. Since such revelation ended with the closing of the biblical canon, God's will for today for his people confronting evil is: **All resistance, all the time.**

BIBLICAL RESISTANCE TO EVIL

The Bible overflows with instances of holy resistance, not resignation, to evil. While we may not resist God's ordinances like civil government (Rom. 13:2), we repeatedly encounter instances of the godly opposing, resisting, and vanquishing evil. Noah resisted his godless antediluvian contemporaries. Abraham pursued, overtook, and spoiled Lot's captors. Moses, Joshua, and the judges resisted the Jews' Canaanite enemies. David resisted the blaspheming Goliath. Elijah resisted the apostate King Ahab and his reprobate wife Jezebel. The old covenant prophets resisted both errant Israel and the depraved nations surrounding it. Jesus came resisting the satanic works of demon possession and sickness as well as the false teaching of the Pharisees and Sadducees. The apostles resisted Christ-denying Judaism and an imperious Rome. Paul resisted the Judaizers. No book in the Bible reflects resistance theology more than Revelation: against both unbelieving Judaism and imperial Rome, both of which God promised to crush — and did, in fact, crush (Rev. 11:15–19; 18:1–19:21).[3]

RESTORING RESISTANCE THEOLOGY

Ours is a time of rampant apostasy, both in church and culture, and this evil fosters resignation among many Christians. They throw up their hands in despair: "What use is resistance? Who knows? Maybe all of this evil God's will." This is a fatal, and faithless, reaction. Evil is never God's will. David Wells writes:

> [A]ccepting the status quo or "life as it is" (i.e., accepting the inevitability of the way things are in life) is to surrender a biblical view of God. This resignation of what is abnormal contains a hidden, unrecognized assumption that God's power to change the world, to overcome Evil with Good, will not be actualized.[4]

The fact that God has chosen to "take his time" in fulfilling his plans with the world[5] and, therefore, in crushing evil, should never lead us to assume he is tolerant toward evil and that we can, as a result, resign ourselves to it. Our task is to separate from and expose and oppose evil. "Resist the devil and he will flee from you" (Jas. 4:7).

"Those who forsake the law," writes Solomon, "praise the wicked, [b]ut such as keep the law contend with them" (Prov. 28:4). "And have no fellowship with the unfruitful works of darkness, but rather expose them" (Eph. 5:11). I draw your attention to the striking fact (noted in the previous chapter) that we are required not merely to avoid evil, but also expose it. We are commanded to battle the lawless around us. Resistance, not resignation.

CONCLUSION

God's objective in his Son's redemptive work is to crush the serpent's head by, first, saving sinners, humans created in his image, and, second, by saving the world from the poisonous consequences of humanity's sin. But this salvation necessitates confrontation, and confrontation requires resistance.

Roe v. Wade, Obergefell, Cultural Marxism, pornography, pride, multiculturalism, extramarital sex, covetousness, Darwinism, prayerlessness, ideological feminism, unbelief, and a host of other cultural sins plague our families, churches, and society. We dare not resign ourselves to them. As long as God doesn't resign himself to sin, we cannot. Bold resistance theology is the calling of the hour.

A CURSE ON ABORTICIDE

*E*very January many churches in the United States highlight God's truth as it relates to preborn children, notably in memory of *Roe v. Wade*, the January 22, 1973 Supreme Court decision legalizing abortion.

Actually the term *abortion* includes the definition of "the expulsion of a fetus from the uterus by natural causes before it is able to survive independently," denoting what is today termed miscarriage. This is not what most people mean when they use the word abortion, however. They mean the intentional termination of human pregnancy, abortion's primary, but not exclusive, definition.

A more suitable term for that intentional act is aborticide,[1] which is a perfectly legitimate English word and enjoys the rhetorical benefit of similarity to homicide, infanticide, suicide, regicide, and other words that denote the willful deprivation of human life. It's a word that supporters of the act likely deplore for precisely the same reason that opponents would prefer it. Supporters want attention deflected from the (im)moral implications of the act and redirected to the benefits to the pregnant woman ("a woman's right to her own body," etc.).

The Christian verdict on aborticide derives from the Bible, which clearly, if not explicitly, condemns it. All intentional deprivation of judicially innocent human life is murder (Gen. 9:6). Human life begins at conception (Jud. 16:17; Ps. 139:13–18; Jer. 1:5; Lk. 1:15). Therefore, aborticide is murder.

More specifically, biblical law requires compensation for a miscarriage unintentionally precipitated by violent human action (Ex. 21:22). Even if the child is miscarried as a result of violent actions that did not intend that fatal loss, the violent are guilty of what we term these days manslaughter (not fetus-slaughter).

A human fetus is a human, created in God's image, entitled to full legal protection.

Legalized aborticide, therefore, is nothing short of legalized murder, not materially different from Nazi leglislation legalizing the extermination of Jews or Marxist laws allowing the liquidation of capitalists.

ABORTICIDE AND THE SEXUAL REVOLUTION

Aborticide is not a solitary horror foisted by political elites on a reluctant populace. While this act is nearly as old as sinful humanity, it became a sociopolitical policy in the West only after the 60's Sexual Revolution since aborticide is, in Mary Eberstadt's language, contraception's backup plan.[2] It is this fact, and likely this fact alone, that accounts for the gradual reduction in aborticide: as contraception becomes more effective and widespread, aborticide decreases. This reduction should furnish cold comfort, however, since it almost surely means that most aborted babies are unwanted residue from illicit and self-centered sexual gratification. In short, the current reduction of aborticide does not signal increased respect for human life — quite the opposite.

A figure at which neutral investigations arrived for acts of aborticide performed in the United States since 1973 is 50 million. To set this figure in context, Hitler exterminated 6 million Jews. Stalin murdered 20 million of his countrymen. Mao may have murdered as many as 70 million. The number of acts of aborticide just in the United States since 1973 boggles the mind, and by these standards the product of the aborticide industry in the United States is nothing less than human holocaust.

ABORTICIDE AND WRATH

It also invites God's judgment. Spilling innocent blood brings God's anger to a boiling point. Habakkuk 2:8 is entirely typical of many warnings in the Old Testament prophets to both the Jews and the surrounding nations:

> *Because you have plundered many nations, all the remnant of the peoples shall plunder you, for the blood of man and violence to the earth, to cities and all who dwell in them.*

God measures out his wrath on a nation and culture that unrepentantly sheds innocent blood, and, while God is longsuffering, it is incredulous to believe that our nation will escape God's judgment if we do not repent — and perhaps even if we do repent (2 Chr. 34:14–33). The blood of preborn innocents, like that of Abel's (Gen. 4:10), cries from the ground for God's holy vengeance.

For this reason also, praying for God's wrath on the perpetrators of this holocaust is not merely appropriate, but imperative (Rev. 6:9–11). As Kemper Krabb's haunting lyric "A Malediction" intones:

> The judges sat outside the law
> And in their pride no evil saw
> In setting teeth to Satan's jaw
> And feeding him our children
> A curse a curse the Law it cries
> A curse a curse on mankind's pride
> A curse on him who would deny
> God's image in mankind[3]

To invoke God's wrath on unrepentant murderers of judicially innocent children is to invoke his tender grace and mercy on the precious lives of preborn children whom they would, if unmolested, also snuff out. Alternatively, to shy from such imprecations under the motivation of sensitivity to butchers of babes is to twist the justice of God and turn his grace into lasciviousness (Jude 1:4).

All followers of Jesus Christ who, therefore, love his holy law and mercy and grace and justice must beg God to grant repentance to our blood-soaked nation — and level his wrath against those lawless judges and unrepentant aborticide providers who "set their teeth to Satan's jaw and feed him our children."

To do less is a cruelty to the most vulnerable among us, even if marinated in misguided piety.

BIBLICAL SEXUALITY, SIMPLY EXPLAINED

We live in unprecedented times of sexual chaos and apostasy. Sexual depravity has infected the world since the fall of humanity, but today we witness not just the wholesale abandonment of creational sexual norms but also the extensive theoretical justification of that abandonment. Modern man wants his sexual depravity and is willing to invent a sophisticated rationale for it — and for how any alternative to the depravity is retrogressive and abnormal. Tragically this ideational perversion isn't limited to the pagan-secular culture but has poisoned the church.

To be a faithful Christian in contemporary culture is to be aware of the Bible's teaching on sexuality and to live according to it. To turn our backs on biblical sexual ethics is to invite a life of heartache and destruction. In our present situation, a summary of the leading points of the biblical teaching on sex should be a welcome contribution.

TWO SEXES

First, God created the sexes: two sexes, and only two, male and female (Gen. 1:27). Both were created in God's image. Woman as the wife was fashioned from man's very body in order to be in the closest possible proximity to him physically, spiritually, emotionally and in every other way. Her chief calling is to assist him in their God-given task of stewardship-dominion over God's creation (Gen. 1:28b–29). While from creation she is subject to his loving, self-sacrificial authority (subject to her husband's authority, not the authority of men in general, a too infrequently recognized distinction), she's in no way inferior to him in her being. She's not a lower order of creature but is equal to her husband in her being. She is his partner in their calling, compensating for his lack and he compensating for hers. Marriage is a partnership.[1]

SEX FOR MARRIAGE

Second, sexual intercourse is reserved exclusively for marriage (Heb. 13:4). A big (though not only) objective for marriage is the propagation of a godly human race (Gen. 1:28a; Mal. 2:15). The logic of God's sexual law seems clear: (1) God wants one man to be committed to one woman for one lifetime, and sexual intercourse as the most intimate act of marriage exhibits that commitment more than any other way except surrendering one's very life (Eph. 5:25, 28). Extramarital sex undermines the lifelong commitment of the one man to the one woman God has given him, and vice versa. (2) Since procreation is a primary objective of intercourse, God's ideal plan is for children to be reared for him in a stable family with a father and mother (Eph. 6:1–3). Extramarital sex often produces extramarital children not formally tied to a single marriage and its loving nourishment. Christian sexual ethics starts with this law: all legitimate sex is marital sex.

INTERCOURSE A DELIGHTFUL BLESSING

Third, sexual intercourse is in no way sinful or even a concession to sin, but a delightful gift from God. The writer of Hebrews (13:4) states, "Marriage is honorable among all, and the bed [sexual intercourse] undefiled; but fornicators and adulterers God will judge." The book of Song of Solomon is a tender, sometimes erotic, love song between a man and woman as they prepare for marriage. There's not a trace of moral self-consciousness about marital sexual intercourse. It's true that the church fathers often had a diminished view of sex and the human body, but this was due to the influence of Gnostic and pagan Greco-Roman ideas. They didn't get this conviction from the Bible, which depicts marital intercourse as beautiful, delightful, and holy.

REPUGNANT SEXUALITY

Fourth, certain specific forms of sexual intercourse are especially repellant. These include homosexuality (Lev. 18:23; 20:13), bestiality (Lev. 20:15–16), and incest (Lev. 18:6f.). Homosexuality is repugnant because it involves intercourse with creatures too much alike. Bestiality is repellant because it involves intercourse with creatures too different. Incest is offensive because, like homosexuality, it involves intercourse with creatures too much alike (linked via marriage). The old covenant (Jewish) civil penalty for these violations (like adultery [Lev. 20:20]) was death (Lev. 20:13). That's how seriously God takes these violations of sexual ethics. While no nation is covenanted to God in civil law in the same way ancient Israel was, the new covenant era equally prohibits these sins.

NEW TESTAMENT SEXUAL NORMS

In confirming the ethics of the Old Testament community (Mt. 5:18–19), our Lord laid down broad ethical norms for sexuality in the New Testament church. His teaching comes in two contexts. The first is divorce. Jesus declares that divorce is not permissible except on the ground of sexual immorality (*porneia*, Mt. 5:32; 19:9). Adultery, of course, is a subset of sexual immorality in which at least one of the participants is married. Jesus corrected false interpretations of the Old Testament about divorce, but he confirmed its prohibition of all sexual immorality.

In the second context, our Lord declares that it is the heart, not the body, that spawns sins like "evil thoughts, murders, adulteries, fornications, thefts, false witness, blasphemies" (Mt. 15:19). Our problem is not our bodies or the external world as such, but our sin, which resides deep in our heart. In both cases, Jesus confirms the Old Testament standard that sex is reserved for marriage.

SEX THAT EXCLUDES FROM THE KINGDOM

The apostle Paul elaborates on this inherited revelation in speaking particularly to the primitive churches. Two passages are especially pertinent. In 1 Cor. 6:9–11 he writes:

> Do you not know that the unrighteous will not inherit the kingdom of God? Do not be deceived. Neither fornicators, nor idolaters, nor adulterers, nor homosexuals, nor sodomites, nor thieves, nor covetous, nor drunkards, nor revilers, nor extortioners **will inherit the kingdom of God**. And such were some of you. But you were washed, but you were sanctified, but you were justified in the name of the Lord Jesus and by the Spirit of our God. (emphasis supplied)

The second is Galatians 5:19–21:

> Now the works of the flesh are evident, which are: adultery, fornication, uncleanness, lewdness, idolatry, sorcery, hatred, contentions, jealousies, outbursts of wrath, selfish ambitions, dissensions, heresies, envy, murders, drunkenness, revelries, and the like; of which I tell you beforehand, just as I also told you in time past, that **those who practice such things will not inherit the kingdom of God**. (emphasis supplied)

Both passages are striking in that Paul declares that specific, unrepentant sins exclude one from the kingdom of God. Those sins include (but are no means limited to) sexual immorality in general and impurity, sensuality, orgies, adultery, and homosexuality in particular.

Paul's point is quite clear: those whose lives are dominated by these sins (as well as specific non-sexual sins) have no part in Christ's kingdom.

Note that Paul goes on to write, "And such were some of you. But you were washed, but you were sanctified, but you were justified in the name of the Lord Jesus and by the Spirit of our God" (1 Cor. 9:11). Some of his Corinthian readers had been sexually immoral but had been washed of this sin (and others). They were declared righteous on the basis of the atoning work of Jesus through the power of the Holy Spirit. Can the sexually immoral be Christians? Yes, but they must leave their sexual immorality behind.

Nor does Paul indicate that that these sins may never creep back into the believer's life. The apostle who wrote Romans 6–8 would hardly suggest that sin no longer has a place in the Christian's life at all, which demands a continual spiritual struggle. But it is a struggle that Christians are expected gradually to overcome in the Holy Spirit's power, and if one professes faith but drifts back into an unrepentant, sin-dominated life, he can expect nothing but spiritual death (Rom. 6:21; 8:6, 9, 13). Let me state Paul's reasoning starkly: if you live in unrepentant sexual immorality, you can't be a Christian. Your destiny is hell. The fact that this comment might sound jarring shows just how far the church has drifted from biblical sexual ethics.

In broad outline, biblical sexual ethics are unmistakably clear. The problem isn't lack of clarity in the Bible; it's lack of fidelity in the church.

THREE AXIOMS ON HOMOSEXUALITY IN THE CHURCH

First, we should have great pity, but also a measure of respect, for those who practice or champion homosexuality and who, understanding its incompatibility with the Faith, publicly abandon Christianity and the church. They understand and act on the principles involved. However, we should view with contempt and suspicion those claiming to be Christians who practice and champion homosexuality while remaining within the church. Some such lay members are simply confused, but the agenda leaders are not. Their attempt to deconstruct the Faith within the walls of the church is a form of subversion and betrayal, and they should be expelled with extreme prejudice if they refuse to repent. You can be a bold, practicing homosexual or a champion of homosexuality, or you can be a biblical Christian. You cannot be both.

Second, all forms of extramarital sex are sinful. The heterosexual sin on which the modern church is most mute is premarital sex. Somehow church leaders have gotten the idea that young single adults should be expected to fornicate until they are married, but when married, should remain faithful to their spouse. There isn't a dime's difference, however, between the sinfulness of adultery and that of non-marital fornication.

But, third, there is much more than a dime's difference between heterosexual violations and homosexuality. Extramarital heterosexual sex between consenting adults is flatly sinful, but it is a violation of God's law within his ordered creation. It is an *ordered* sin. Homosexuality, however, is a contra-creational and contra-cosmic sin. It attempts to overthrow the sexual order of the cosmos. It is, therefore, a *dis*ordered sin. For this reason, it is wrong for Christian leaders to scold us critics of homosexuality with the idea that, "Well, all extramarital sex is bad, and [heterosexual] adultery is just as bad as homosexuality." No. They are both sinful, but heterosexual fornication and adultery do not attempt to overthrow the cosmos. Homosexuality is high-handed subversion of God's ordered universe.

REFORMING ONLY THE FAMILY AND CHURCH WON'T SUFFICE

We live in transformational times for the Christian faith. The last vestiges of Christian culture are waning. Until recent decades, Christianity shaped the West. This doesn't mean all or even most people were Christian; it means that the basic Christian gospel and ethic had historically rooted society's institutions, and were recognized by most people (including unbelievers) to do this. At worst, the West was "vaguely Christian" in most people's minds.[1]

THE GRAND CHANGE

All that has changed. Today, Christian businesses are assaulted for simply acting on biblical, family truth, which had been practiced freely in the U. S. for over 240 years. Church attendance is declining. Millennials reared in the faith are leaving it by many thousands; they are more likely to be "Social Justice Warriors" than soldiers for Jesus Christ. Same-sex "marriage" is increasingly accepted among evangelicals. The social elites embrace and impose Cultural Marxism.[2] This is the ideology that adapts Marx's classical ideas to the West. Armed revolution won't work here, but the "long march through the institutions" will — and has: All hierarchies are evil. Individual autonomy, guaranteed by an iron-clad state, is the highest good. The courts must be used not to lay down impartial legal decisions but to secure the "just society," as interpreted by "progressive" dogma. The previously marginalized in society (women, homosexuals, criminals, the poor, racial minorities, children, the disabled) must be exalted and championed, and the previously exalted must be humiliated and brought low: Christians, white males, fathers, the wealthy, and intact traditional families.

CHRISTIANS CONFUSED

Amid this apostasy, unprecedented in the U. S., older, devout Christians are at a loss. The world is shifting under their feet. The 2016 election of Donald Trump was a welcome respite for them, not because his life and language have been exemplary, but because he represented a bulwark against this tide of politically correct unbelief. They still feel beleaguered. What is the remedy? Many are calling for revival and reform in the church and family. This idea is understandable. The church is Christ's body in the earth. The church is the custodian of orthodoxy (right belief).

The church monopolizes the sacraments or ordinances. The church holds the earthly keys to the kingdom: who is a Christian and who isn't. There is no Christianity, no Christian culture, without the church. The family is similar, and even more foundational than the church. The family is a creational norm. It was around before the Fall. Had the Fall never happened, there would have been a family, though not a church or state, at least not as we know them in God's redemptive order. To preserve the family is to preserve God's basic unit of human society. To lose the family is to lose the human building block of God's created order. This is what is new: *self-consciously anti-Christian culture.*

FULL-FLEDGED REFORMATION

But society is much larger than these institutions, and therefore the apostasy of today's world is much larger. Reforming only the family and church won't suffice. It's necessary, but not sufficient. Think of it this way. Almost *everything* Christians encounter when they leave the safe haven of the family and church is at war with almost *everything* they encounter within the family and church. Family and church teach: "Put God first. Jesus is Lord. Obey the Bible. Trust God to provide. Sacrifice for others. Marriage is sacred. Sex is for marriage. Be careful of your words. There is a Final Judgment." The surrounding culture teaches: "Put yourself first. You are lord. Obey your own impulses. You must make your own success happen. Your priorities are most important. Marriage is an informal, temporary arrangement. Sex is a malleable social construct. Say whatever you want whenever you want. You'll never be required to give a final account for how you live on earth." Of course, an anti-Christian worldview isn't new. It's been pervasive in other times and cultures. What *is* new in the West is that this secular worldview has consciously abandoned Christianity and Christian culture. In other words, what is historically unprecedented is a civilization that in sequence has consciously (1) embraced Christianity, (2) abandoned Christianity, and (3) embraced anti-Christianity. This is what is new: self-consciously anti-Christian culture. This is what devout Christians must contend with.

INDIVIDUAL CHRISTIANS NOT ENOUGH

It's impossible for a virile Christianity to survive for long *institutionally* in such a hostile climate. Yes, devout individuals can. Noah, Moses, Daniel, the apostles, and the primitive Christians did. But since Christianity by its nature is a world-dominating Faith, it suffers greatly when its cultural surroundings are not Christian. This is one chief reason that so many children reared in devout Christian families are drifting from Jesus Christ. The Faith in which they were reared is an inherently cultural Faith calculated by God himself to be reinforced in all of life. The radical disconnect between a God-loving family and church on the one hand and God-defying popular music and education and science and technology and art and architecture on the other creates spiritual schizophrenia.

Because today's secular culture is almost all-consuming, Christian young people are easy prey. It is a well-intentioned, self-assuring error to assume that if we can just get the church fired up for God and restore godliness to the family, we can restore a large number of devout Christians and Christian culture. A plethora of devout Christians require a cultural canopy of Christianity, which reinforces *everywhere* the most basic Christian belief: "Jesus is Lord!"

LIBERAL CHRISTIANITY ISN'T

One of the leading American theologians of the 20th century was J. Gresham Machen. One of his most famous books was *Christianity and Liberalism*.[1] He argues that theological liberalism, sometimes called modernism at the time, isn't a new version of Christianity. Rather, it's not Christianity at all. It's another religion altogether.

Liberalism consisted of a fusion of 18th-century rationalism (man's reason is the final arbiter of truth) and 19th century romanticism (man's experience is the final arbiter of truth). The foundational spirit of liberalism is simple: Christianity must conform to the temper of the times. The Bible and Christian dogma are not finally authoritative. Man's reason and experience in the modern world, particularly as exhibited in science, are finally authoritative.

Perhaps the single greatest source of all liberalism was the greatest Enlightenment philosopher of all, Immanuel Kant.[2] Kant believed that man can gain knowledge only from his senses interacting with pre-established categories of human thought. Man can know nothing of certainty about God or the spiritual world. Man's mind isn't *constructed* to know God. Kant did not deny God existed. He denied, however, that we could have reliable knowledge about God. Kant's influence on theological liberals meant that they were free to invent the kind of God and the kind of Christian Faith they wanted to have.

This last point is liberalism in a nutshell.

The early liberals questioned the authenticity of the Bible's text, the orthodox Trinity, the biblical account of miracles, the deity of Jesus Christ, and other central truths of Christianity.

THE NEW LIBERALISM

Contemporary liberals have changed. They haven't changed liberalism's guiding principle (they still often deny the doctrines early liberals denied about the Faith); but they have changed what they emphasize in denying. Because the temper of the times has changed, they have been obliged to change.

The real issues for them today are sexual autonomy, moral relativism, and Cultural Marxism. In other words, the very things popular in the surrounding apostate culture. If the credo of liberalism is conforming the Faith to the contemporary world, liberals must always be inherently worldly.

Just as the tenets of early liberalism with which Machen interacted were diametrically opposed to Christianity, so the guiding beliefs of today's liberalism are. The Bible supports sexual fidelity (sexual intercourse between a married man and woman), not sexual autonomy. The Bible presupposes God's revelation as final truth, and it obviously cannot permit moral relativism. The Bible dictates hierarchies in all areas of life, starting with God's hierarchy over man. There's no place for the leveling of all hierarchies, which is what Cultural Marxism is all about.

MACHEN 2.0

Machen understood that liberalism was not disputing important but secondary issues of the Faith, like the sacraments or ordinances, church polity, the specifics of biblical prophecy, the sign gifts, and so on. Rather, liberalism cut the heart out of the Faith — the inspiration and infallibility of the Bible, the virgin birth and deity and bodily resurrection of Jesus Christ, and his substitutionary atonement on the Cross. When you don't have these, it's not orthodox Christianity you lose. It's Christianity you lose.

The reason many Christians are confused as to how to classify today's liberals is that they've not until recently encountered professed Christians who aren't boldly denying the Apostles Creed but who are denying tenets of biblical teaching that the church everywhere until recently has affirmed. Those teachings include marriage as between one man and one woman, homosexuality as sin, abortion as murder, and radical sexual egalitarianism as contra-creational. Today's liberals deny them for the same reason: the Bible's teaching doesn't fit the temper of the age. Until recent decades (or years), no one, not even the early liberals, would have thought of questioning these biblical truths. Even if we agree with Machen about the early liberals, what should we say about modern liberals? We should say the same thing Machen said: liberalism isn't Christianity. Churches that establish a policy accepting unrepentant homosexuals or same-sex "marriage" or encouraging abortion or radical sexual egalitarianism are not Christian churches.

Why? Because Jesus and Paul and Peter and John would not have considered same-sex "marriage" less evil or dangerous (Rom. 1:18–32) than (for example) the Gnostic heresy that Jesus did not come in the flesh (2 Jn. 7). Not all false teaching striking at the core of Christianity is found in the Apostles Creed. Why? Because no one at the time the Creed was developed would have dreamed of assuming that the Bible would permit, for instance, homosexuality or radical sexual egalitarianism. If anything, this shows that the violations of today's liberals might be even more destructive than heresies of the early centuries of the church since at the time nobody, including the heretics, would have even considered them. Arianism (the Son of God is a created being) is a pernicious heresy, but no Arian would have supported same-sex "marriage."

Machen 2.0 would say what Machen 1.0 said: teachings that strike at the very heart of Christianity so distort it that if unchecked they produce another religion.

That religion is not Christianity.

ARMED TO THE TEETH, PACIFIST TO THE CORE

The Christian Faith is marinated in optimism because the Bible is hopeful from cover the cover. The biblical worldview is based on creation-fall-redemption.[1] The catastrophe of sin is bookended by a hope-drenched creation and the restored and enhanced creation known as redemption.

God created a lush, splendorous world of hope and joy and optimism. Right after man sinned in submitting to satanic rebellion, God promised a Redeemer who would crush the serpent's head (Gen. 3:15). God later destroyed the depraved antediluvian world, but re-launched with Noah. Later, God called out Abram and launched a nation, promising him a great seed and land. The Jews tragically departed from their loving Lord and his law, but he sent his own Son to them, and to die for the sins of the world. In his death, our Lord beat down the "principalities and powers," the satanic forces arrayed against God (Col. 2:13–15). In his resurrection he ascended to his heavenly throne from which he is progressively beating down the forces of evil by the power of the gospel (Ac. 2:29–36; 1 Cor. 15:20–26). The book of Revelation is a dramatic vision of the triumph of the Lamb over all his enemies. You cannot understand the Bible unless you understand its hopeful, optimistic message.

PESSIMISTIC PACIFISTS

Unfortunately many Christians today seem to have missed the optimistic arc of the Bible's message. They either believe we are living in "the last days" and can expect nothing but increasing apostasy. Or else they embrace conspiracy theories that see sinister, secret forces everywhere preventing the gospel from succeeding. For still others the daily challenges of rearing children in a depraved culture, trying to stay current on bills, coping with broken family relations and friendships, and coming to terms with illness and death nearly overwhelm them. Since this pessimism is irreconcilable with the promises of the Bible, it can only mean that they (we) are living in unbelief. To trust and act on the promises of the word is to live in consistent optimism.

INDIVIDUAL VICTORY

God promises victory in our individual lives. In Romans 6 and 8 Paul makes clear that by union with the crucified and risen Christ we are freed from the power of sin. Paul's agonizing cry in Romans 7 over the power of indwelling sin is sometimes wrongly interpreted to refute the message of hopeful victory. He is not describing normative Christian living but rather anomalous Christian living (perhaps even moralistic non-Christian living). The standard Christian life is one of victory over sin, though never perfectly in this life. We can and should live in persistent victory over the power of sin. Take hope: you are not destined to enslavement to covetousness or lust or porn or anxiety or alcohol or drugs. There is no sin you *must* commit. The Holy Spirit has freed us for consistent victory.

FAMILY VICTORY

God promises victory in our family. The family is under unremitting attack today, and Christians often abandon hope for an intact, joyous, multigenerational Christian family. But God's promises are clear (Ps.

128; Pr. 11:21), and despite great failures in a marriage and children spiritually adrift, those promises hold secure to those who claim them in simple faith. If your marriage is faltering and your children failing, remind God of his promises, and redouble your commitment to obedience, expecting an entire family devoted to him.

CHURCH VICTORY

God promises victory to the church. The most obvious one is in Matthew 16:17–19: the gates of hell (or the grave) won't prevail against the church. The Bible does not predict that the church will fail in its task to disciple the nations. The lamentable state of the church in the West today is no predictor of its future. Pray and expect God to raise up great men and women of faith who will declare the gospel of Jesus Christ in power, edify the saints, and call the world to account for its sins: "The power is available, but the church seems in large measure to believe that the power does not exist, or she lacks the will to observe the necessary laws."[2]

CULTURAL VICTORY

Finally, God promises victory in our culture. Even Christians optimistic about victory in the individual life and family and church often draw the line here. But the culture-victory promises are just as prominent as the others. The knowledge of the Lord will cover the earth as the waters cover the sea (Hab. 2:14). The end of all things will not come until the presently reigning Christ subdues all his enemies (1 Cor. 15:23–25). The victory comes not after the Second Advent, but before. It is a victory of the present age.[3]

Christians today are conditioned for defeat. For 100 years they've been told that they cannot expect consistent victory over sin. That Christian families cannot expect to turn out better than non-Christian families. That the church will grow progressively weaker over time. That the world is destined to rush toward depravity before the Second Coming. And that Christians can do nothing to impede defeat on all earthly fronts. This view is poppycock, rank unbelief. In the 1930's France's intellectuals and schools and famous writers, the horrors of World War I fresh in their minds, churned out pacifism. France became a hotbed of defeatism.[4] Winston Churchill wrote: "France, though armed to the teeth, is pacifist to the core." It was no surprise that France folded like an unpegged tent in a windstorm when the Germans invaded.

Christians "are armed to the teeth [but] pacifist to the core." Our King owns everything, but an alien, Satan, has subversively commandeered part of his domain, the earth, and set up a rival kingdom. We are the King's citizen-army, commissioned to expel the usurper. That's what the great commission is: The marching orders of the church. Satan is a squatter. He and his minions sneaked onto God's property and erected little shantytowns and bought some BB guns and claim to be taking over. What a pitiful lot they are! We, conversely, enjoy the irrepressible promises of God's word, the relentless power of the Spirit, and the authority of the risen Lord behind us. Let us march boldly in faith and hope and optimism, expecting nothing less than unconditional victory.

CREATION: THE EVANGELICAL FAILURE

If you wonder why too many evangelicals are caving in to same-sex "marriage," or "attraction," surrogacy, "gender fluidity," and transgenderism, part of the fault lies in the DNA of evangelicalism itself. Evangelicals champion the biblical evangel, the good news that Jesus Christ died for our sins and rose from the dead so that sinners can be saved. This is their paradigmatic specialty and we should thank God that they have enjoyed great success over the last two centuries.[1]

THE CREATIONAL MARGINALIZATION

But with this specialization has come the marginalization of other parts of the Bible, notably creation. Not that evangelicals deny creation. They are often at the forefront defending six-day creation, the historicity of Adam and Eve, and the universal flood. However, they have tended not to integrate creation into their worldview. Worse: they have not understood that creation is the foundation of the gospel. This is very easy to prove, if you think about it. The gospel offers salvation from sin, but what is sin? It is a violation of God's law (1 Jn. 3:4). But how did this violation come about? It came about as result of man's distortion of creation. Genesis chapters 1–2 lay out creational laws, or norms. These include the Creator-creature distinction, humanity made in God's image, the distinction between man and woman within that single divine image, the fruitfulness imperative, the cultural mandate, the Sabbath, and the goodness of creation itself. We might call these the creational OS: operating system. This is how God designed the cosmos to work.

And it is within just this operating system that the gospel software works. Sin introduced a virus into that operating system. The object of the gospel is incrementally to eliminate that virus. The virus doesn't obliterate the operating system, but it does impair it. The gospel is God's hunt-and-destroy-the-virus mission.

Evangelicals have tended, however, to internalize, privatize, and Gnosticize the gospel. The gospel is chiefly about getting sinners forgiven by God and fellowshipping with him and taking them to heaven. It's understandable that, in this telling, addressing same-sex "marriage" might be a tangent to keep the church away from the gospel. Taking on surrogacy, egg harvesting, and transhumanism (like Jennifer Lahl's Center of Bioethics and Culture does) is at best a secondary cause and, at worst, a distraction from the church's mission.

But if we understand that the objective of the gospel is the restoration of God's created order, increasing adherence to his creational norms, not just for his glory but for our delight, we will recognize these tasks and many others as well within the framework of the biblical gospel.

THE MEDIATOR OF CREATION

A fundamental theological flaw is at the root of this truncated gospel. Modern evangelicals see Jesus as the mediator of redemption, but seem less interested in him as the mediator of creation. But the Bible plainly teaches both.[2] See what Paul writes in Colossians 1:13–19:

> He [God the Father] has delivered us from the power of darkness and

conveyed us into the kingdom of the Son of His love, in whom we have redemption through His blood, the forgiveness of sins [here's Jesus, the mediator of redemption]. He is the image of the invisible God, the firstborn over all creation. For by Him all things were created that are in heaven and that are on earth, visible and invisible, whether thrones or dominions or principalities or powers. All things were created through Him and for Him. And He is before all things, and in Him all things consist [here's Jesus, the mediator of creation.] And He is the head of the body, the church, who is the beginning, the firstborn from the dead, that in all things He may have the preeminence. For it pleased the Father that in Him all the fullness should dwell, and by Him to reconcile all things to Himself, by Him, whether things on earth or things in heaven, having made peace through the blood of His cross.

For Paul, Jesus' mediation in both creation and redemption work together to convey the fullness of God to and within the cosmos. The Jesus who died on the old rugged cross is the same Jesus who shaped the universe's laws and upholds its existence.

Because evangelicals have embraced a truncated view of the Bible, because they have emphasized the evangel (narrowly construed) as the be-all-and-end-all, they have been willing to sacrifice the more fundamental creational truths on which the true evangel is founded. They didn't set out to do this. And if someone had told them even 20 years ago that they would one day endorse or surrender to "gender fluidity" or same-sex "marriage," they would have scoffed. But their preoccupation with one vital part of the Bible and relative neglect of other vital parts paved the way for these wholesale changes. The seeds of the present compromises were there from the beginning. The neglect wasn't intentional, but it was neglect, and we're now paying a bitter price for it.

The solution to this neglect is a return to a full-orbed robust view of creation and creational norms. Let's preach the Jesus of the old rugged cross and the even older creational Lordship.

THE REVENGE OF THE COSMOS

Carl Henry's 40-year verdict on his small early book *The Uneasy Conscience of Modern Fundamentalism* included the summary: "[T]wo things sometimes surprise me: ... how little I said and how boldly I said it" (*Theology, News and Notes*, December, 1987, p. 3). I had a similar experience reading Christopher Wiley's *The Household and the War for the Cosmos: Recovering a Christian Vision for the Family* (Canon Press, 2019). It is a brief, bold book. Wiley argues that the Christian household (not identical to the modern deracinated "nuclear family") is at the center of God's original cosmological configuration. The fact that this household is hierarchical (the father, for example, is the "middleman of the cosmos . . . stand[ing] between his household and heaven, representing each to the other" [p. 76]) will incite outrage not only from secular egalitarians but also many churchmen (I apologize: churchpersons) for whom individual autonomy is an ultimate human right. Wiley, a Presbyterian pastor, nonetheless sees the family as the center of God's plan for humanity and argues bluntly that "the Bible is a kind of handbook for households" (p. 5). Which is to say that the household isn't just at the center of the cosmos. It's also at the center of Christianity itself.

Of course, none of this means all is well with the household in our fallen postmodern world. All to the contrary. We are living amid cultural collapse. Wiley contends that this collapse is largely the effect of household collapse, offering five evidences: (1) marriage has been reduced to a lifestyle choice; (2) children are increasingly believed to be useless or even bad to have; (3) post-familialism is on the rise; (4) we're sliding into socialism; and (5) Christians are losing the ability to think like Christians.

PRIVATIZED CHRISTIANITY

The collapse has been abetted by a highly privatized conservative Christianity that gained ascendancy as early as the 18th century. Well-intentioned revivalists like John Wesley and George Whitefield had reduced the cosmological faith of Christianity to a private, heart affair. No Christian at that time, least of all the evangelical revivalists themselves, could have dreamed that this individualization could lead to a modern radical individualism that undermines the household. For the household is not a collection of autonomous individuals. It is a divinely constructed reality at the center of the cosmos. By reducing the Faith to heart religion, the well-meaning revivalists unwittingly decontextualized the individual from the cosmic order within which he was intended to live and move and have his being. Central to that order is the household.

But the household's most pernicious enemy isn't human. Satan himself is warring on the cosmic order. The strategy of his contragodly principalities and powers is to undermine and subvert God's cosmological order. That means, of course, destabilizing and eventually destroying the household. The task of Christians is to restore that household according to God's law.

THE COSMIC ORDER

This broad, sweeping vision sets Wiley squarely within the Genesis 1–2 camp and not the Genesis 3 camp of modern evangelicalism.[1] The Genesis 1–2 camp sees God's created cosmic order and its development by godly humans as their chief calling (the "cultural mandate"). The Genesis 3 Christians perceive God's work on the earth as personal redemption, rescuing sinners from judgment and calling them into the church and to greater sanctification.

The Genesis 1–2 Christians, by contrast, don't disagree with the content of this vision, but they see it as subordinate to the larger Genesis 1–2 vision. Because the cosmological household stands squarely within the Genesis 1–2 camp, Genesis 3 Christians are inclined to see Wiley's emphasis as at best secondary and at worst a distraction from what he should really be doing: keeping sinners out of hell and getting them sanctified and ready to meet the Lord. Wiley would likely reply that if you're not a Genesis 1–2 Christian, you won't be able to maintain Genesis 3 Christianity for long. You won't win the gospel war if you abandon the cosmic war.

GUERRILLA PIETY

Wiley offers two strategies for winning that war, by practicing what he calls, in a whiplashing metaphor, guerrilla piety. First, the church must act as it was designed: the household of God, and quit chasing the world and "relevance." The church itself is indispensable to the cosmic hierarchy. Its goal is to "put the benefits of Christ's rule on display for the principalities and power" (p. 120). This advice will not appeal to the pragmatic churchlings among us for whom a Christianized version of the latest cultural kitsch is agenda item #1.

THE FULCRUM OF THE COSMOS

Second, Christians must recognize that "the household is the fulcrum of the cosmos" (p. 121). Wiley offers as evidence a seemingly benign point that actually delivers a powerful punch: "The reason households have leverage is that they are natural" (Ibid.). What makes this argument potent is its radical antithesis to the present privileging of socially constructed reality. Nature (creation, cosmos) doesn't matter. It gets in the way of human imagination and therefore reality must change: reality isn't what it used to be.[2] If you want to redefine the household as two lesbians, three toddlers, and a border collie, more power to you. If you want to transform yourself into a dragon, don't let the cosmos get in your way. Reality is an optional impediment to be pulverized to make way for the creative, autonomous self. This is the gospel of cultural Gnosticism.

Wiley understands that the Satanic assault on the cosmic family will finally fail, because it is a war on reality. If you try to break God's physical cosmic laws like gravity and thermodynamics, you'll end up breaking yourself. If you try to break God's institutional cosmic laws for the household, you'll get the same result.

In the current war over the cosmos, Wiley urges Christians to stand with the cosmos. That means: stand with the household.

The cosmos, like Father Time, is still undefeated.

THE THINNESS OF THE CHURCH

Today's church is increasingly thin.[1] It has little substance. It blows about with every wind of doctrine (Eph. 4:14). It drifts from fad to fad, from kitsch to kitsch, from celebrity to celebrity. It chases the latest cultural prostitute. It is the laughingstock of the depraved society it so slavishly imitates. The church no longer commands serious attention because it does not take itself seriously as God's redeemed body in the world. The pastor was once looked to as the moral and intellectual leader of the community. Now he is disparaged (often accurately) as a zealous know-nothing and consummate fundraiser. The church is superficial, consumerist, self-absorbed, mercurial. Thin indeed.

THIN PROGRAMS

What are the marks of a thin church? First, a thin church **expands its programs and contracts its godliness**. It is forever appointing committees and calling meetings to "strategize" about how to enlist more attendees by catering to their niche consumption addictions: MOPS, Super Singles, Celebrate Recovery. Sermons are geared to personal fulfillment ("Seven Steps to a Happier Marriage" and "Spiritual Strategies for Achieving Your Life's Goals"). The congregation, suckled on self-help culture, develop "itching ears" (2 Tim. 4:3) to be scratched by spiritual lifestyle coaches meeting a market demand. Members do not live as a covenant community, pouring their lives into one another, but are simply atomistic spiritual consumers plugged into the religious satisfaction generator known as the postmodern church.

THIN LEADERSHIP

Second, a thin church **expects the "senior pastor" to be the company CEO,** driving a growing organization and "plant," preferably incremental building programs. The "executive pastor" is more executive than pastor, perhaps holding an MBA and expected to keep the member-shareholders happy with the bottom line. Feeding the flock is incidental. The thin-church shepherd's job description is beautifying the sheepfold, motivating the other sheep-leaders to keep that flock incessantly active inside the fold, and preserving his own reputation among neighboring shepherds.

THIN MUSIC

Third, a thin church **molds its music around the wider cultural sensibilities.** Ours is an age of radically rhythm-driven and lyrically over-simplistic performance music, and the church is no exception. "In this moment you're right beside me/ You're everywhere, you're in the air that I breathe/ Every morning you keep coming/ The waves of your affection keep washing over me." The Sunday morning laser-light concert showcases the swaying female alto and hipster guitarist, and the congregation haltingly mouths the screen lyrics never intended to be sung by anybody but the gaudy professionals. The music, like our culture, is existential, not majestic.

THIN IDEAS

Fourth, a thin church is **ignorant of or uninterested in the Christian worldview**. The Triune God wishes to transform our lives by transforming our minds (Rom. 12:2), but the thin church is thickly invested in the anti-intellectual temper of the age, preferring emotion, passion, and intuition and bypassing the mind. The unified creation-fall-redemption paradigm of the Bible and its implications for the world are of little interest. While it may stress redemption (narrowly conceived as personal salvation), the church omits biblical creational norms that shape the cosmos. Self-absorbed emotional intensity, sprinkled with churchy Jesus-language, rules the day.

THIN VISION

Fifth, a thin church **ecclesiasticizes the Bible and the Faith**.[2] All the important things happen in the church. The thin church is incestuous. There is no appetite for the Kingdom of God, for pressing the Lordship of Christ in technology, education, the arts, politics, science, and the wider culture — outside the church. That new gaming-addiction recovery program is much, much more important. The thin church equates the church with the Kingdom. Few theological ideas are more dangerous (see chapter 2).

THIN MESSAGE

Sixth, a thin church **refuses to confront the surrounding culture** at the very points at which that culture is assaulting God and his word. The thin church is the cowardly church. Because the Sexual Revolution is the most visible cultural depravity today, it vanquishes the thin church. Premarital sex and same-sex "attraction" must be afforded "safe spaces," either never mentioned, or positively encouraged, for "broken" people who wish to persist in their sin. Under the guise of compassion,[3] the thin church sells biblical truth down the river for a mess of modernist pottage.

THIN SANCTIFICATION

Finally, a thin church **knows nothing of ecclesial sanctification**, growing in grace as a body. The leaders' goal, rather, is to create a product/service that increases breadth, not depth. Long-time members grow uneasy that the sermons are pabulum designed for the merry-go-round of new attendees, but lack any meat to feed the souls of those wishing to move beyond spiritual adolescence (1 Cor. 3:1–2). Covenant, Kingdom, worldview, the cultural mandate, wealth, self-sacrifice, judgment, hospitality, individual and eschatological victory and other vital themes are rarely mentioned. Members trudge ahead as spiritual pygmies, as the church increases its programs and membership.

CONCLUSION

A thick church, in radical contrast, reflects a robust faith. Its leaders are on their face before God and his word. The Triune God, not the apostate culture, sets the church's agenda. They lovingly press the faithful toward greater obedience, greater knowledge, greater faith, and greater expectation. The music is theologically substantial and conveys truth that turns religious backbone into iron. The thick church speaks prophetically for biblical sexual ethics and against the Sexual Revolution. It holds antinomian and spineless politicians accountable to God's standards. This church might be scorned and persecuted by pagans and secularists (and jellyfish Christians), but it is a bright light shining on a hill in a very dark time. To return to the initial metaphor: it is thick, weighty, substantial, a force to be taken with utmost seriousness — including by her Lord.

THE PROGRESSIVES' MARCH TOWARD GOD'S JUDGMENT

"*Liberal*" has become a dirty word in the last few decades, so liberals have latched onto "progressive." After all, who's opposed to progress except hillbilly fundamentalists and head-in-the-sand technophobes? But behind the moniker "progressive" are also deep worldview assumptions. When candidate Barak Obama warned his Democratic audience that the Republicans would "take [them] back to the 1920's," he didn't find it necessary to elaborate. He could assume they embraced the basic progressive presupposition that the measure of linear history is the march of moral improvement. In 2019, our cell phones and cars are superior to those of the past, and so are our political and sexual standards. This is the great premise of modern progressivism: whatever comes later is better.[1]

GENUINE HISTORICAL PROGRESS

This is not only a contemporary idea, but the idea of historical progress was rare in the ancient world. Aside from the Jews, it was almost unheard of. Ancient pagans saw civilization as cyclical: rise, ascendency, prominence, decline, and fall.[2] This view led to pessimism and despair. Christianity inherited from the Jewish faith the belief in incremental progress toward a glorious age to come, ushered in by Messiah, whom they knew to be Jesus of Nazareth. True progress is the fruit of godly faith and obedience. It is social sanctification.

SECULARIZED PROGRESS

The Enlightenment began to secularize the Christian promise of progress. This secularized progress was served up in different forms. In the 19th century Karl Marx theorized that progress in society comes only by the conflict between human classes, but chiefly the bourgeoisie (property owners) and the proletariat (propertyless workers).[3] Today's Cultural Marxists take this a step further: progress is possible not only by economic conflict but also sexual, racial, and regional conflict. This conflict produces the New Man (excuse me: the New Person: the politically correct grammarian thugs must have their say). This development is the sociopolitical counterpart of Darwinism in science. Just as higher species develop by "survival of the fittest," so higher morality develops by contesting and vanquishing traditional morality.

LIBERATION CRUSADES

The battle of the Cultural Marxists (and theirs is the guiding elite sociopolitical vision of our time) is to liberate the West from the "repressive" tendencies of the past, especially the Christian past. This liberation crusade encompasses one sphere after another. For example, in jurisprudence, constitutions must be considered "living" documents, interpreted according to present standards. Why? Because the authors lived in a time when moral standards were inferior. They did not include the right of a mother to abort her unborn child or the right of homosexuals to marry. They didn't know better at the time.

ECONOMIC PROGRESSIVISM

And then consider economics. The free market system on which the U.S. was partly founded presupposes the biblical guarantee of private (or family) property. Private ownership is a God-given right. Progressives are confident that this is a false, naïve assumption. The individual is not important; we now know the collective is what's important. As Marx taught, it's not that the free market is absolutely bad; in fact, capitalism is a stage through which civilization must have travelled. But that stage is over, and we're now on the verge of a higher, greater stage of socialism.

THE PROGRESSIVE CHURCH

Nor has the church been immune from progressivism. The guiding adage of modernism, related to progressivism, is "Make it new!"[4] Every age must be governed by its own, unique views and standards, not those inherited from the past. In the case of Christianity this meant that the old, timeworn Bible must be replaced by human reason and experience, and that the classical creeds and orthodoxy were no longer relevant.[5] In practical terms, this translated into the erasure of sin and judgment, the installation of women pastors, and the introduction of Sunday morning laser-light-show entertainment.

SEXUAL "PROGRESS"

Perhaps the most diabolical instance of progressivism, however, has been the Sexual Revolution launched in the Sixties. It has progressed (= regressed) from miniskirts and premarital sex to gay "marriage" and transgenderism. The Playboy culture and easy availability of condoms were not enough. In fact, they were just the start. The progressivist revolution must devour everything in its path. Its main impediment has been the institution of marriage. The gay "marriage" agenda is not to expand marriage, but to destroy the family. What makes marriage what it is, is the uniqueness of its participants: one man and one woman covenantally committed to one another before God for a lifetime. To redefine marriage is to destroy it. If just any relationship can be marriage, there can be no marriage.

But sexual progressivism will never stop with the abolition of marriage. As Leon Trotsky, Lenin's comrade, claimed, the revolution must be permanent. The next step is progress beyond male and female: God's creation is a barrier to human imagination, so the elites must restructure reality. Creation stands in the way of progress. Reality itself is the enemy. This was the claim of the ancient Gnostics, and it is the program of their 21st century successors.[6] "My male or female body parts assigned at conception and developed in the womb may not prevent me from realizing my dreams of utter sexual autonomy. I am entitled to 'Gender Affirmation Surgery' to make my body conform to my imagination. Sexual progress demands it."

PROGRESS AGAINST THE CREATED ORDER

Progressivism necessitates the eventual overturning of the created order. The goal is not simply rebellion against God's creation; it is the new creation by autonomous man. This goal is satanic. It is materially no different from the Serpent's hiss in Eden: "Eve, God is trying to keep pleasant things from you. Break his unjust order so that you can be truly free."

Because we live in a God-rigged universe, the new Gnostics will not succeed any more than Eve and Adam did, though their rebellion can wreak havoc in the process, just as our first parents' did. Not just the Jews but also the Gentile nations are subject to God's moral law (Is. 13ff.; Rom. 3:19). The progressives might believe that morals are evolving right along with history, but they will be judged by the ancient, unchanging standard of biblical law. This judgment is not limited to eternity, but will arrive in history, just as it did for ancient Egypt, Babylon, Persia, Greece, and Rome (Dan. 2, 7). God will halt the progressives' revolution in its tracks. He will create an earthly

Zion corresponding to the heavenly Zion (Is. 2:1–4; 9:1–7; Heb. 12:18–29). God will throw the unrepentant progressives, today so proud of their moral superiority, into the dustbin of history.

A NOTE ON FAITH, WORKS, AND JUSTIFICATION

A friend recently asked my opinion about a famous Bible teacher charged with heresy because of his view of the relationship between faith and good works. Here is the substance of my response:

I've spent hundreds of hours researching this very topic (exegetical theology, systematic theology, and historical theology), and I wrote two academic dissertations relating to this issue and have finally come to believe that most of our Puritan forefathers understood (or at least expressed) it better than we often do.[1]

The best answer in this case is the simple answer: faith alone saves, but the faith that saves is never alone. We're not saved by works, yet we are never saved without works. God does not look at our good works and justify us, but justification without good works is spurious.

We cast all of our faith, all of our hope, all of our expectations on the crucified and risen Jesus Christ who loved us, and gave himself for us. He accomplished our salvation at Calvary and from the empty tomb. When we are united him by faith (alone), we're also united to resurrection victory, and that victory includes — in fact, necessitates — good works. If works are lacking, this omission only proves that we are not united to the crucified and resurrected Lord.

I've known people to go way, way into the weeds on this issue and come back no better than when they started, and often worse. Eternal life is not a reward for good behavior, but neither can there be a salvation minus good works.

As simple as it may sound, this is a good summary of precisely what I believe the Bible teaches.

CHRISTMAS VERSUS EXCARNATION

*E*very Advent and Christmas season we celebrate the incarnation of our Lord Jesus Christ. Incarnation literally denotes enfleshment. The eternal Son of God assumed humanity as a babe in Bethlehem in order to grow to adulthood and die for the sins of the world. This death and subsequent resurrection, the source of our salvation, presuppose incarnation. Without incarnation, there can be no salvation.

The opposite of incarnation is *excarnation,* a word coined by the Canadian philosopher Charles Taylor[1] to describe the modern inclination to limit all the significant issues of reality to the mind. The body and material world are simply vehicles for reason and imagination. Excarnation is indebted to ancient Gnosticism, the first and most dangerous Christian heresy that afflicts the church and culture down to this very day.[2] While the Bible located the world's ills in human sin, Gnosticism blamed them on creation itself. An ignorant, malign deity (the Demiurge) broke from the true God and created matter, including the human body, contrary to the highest God's desire.

The true God tried to foil the Demiurge by covertly inserting sparks of divinity into the human bodies. To the Gnostics, the Fall is not from righteousness into sin, but from spirit into matter; and salvation is escape from the body and reversion to pure spirit. This means the human body and the material world are a prison from which the enlightened must escape. Jesus came not to save from sin, but to deliver from ignorance and impart knowledge (gnosis), by which the illuminated learn of their true, excarnated destiny.

For Christians, man is rescued by God's Son becoming man in assuming (and dying and rising in) a human body. For Gnostics, man is rescued by escaping from his body, after which the divine spark is released to return to the heavenlies. Man becomes God. Excarnation is the process of man's salvation. This heresy is the antithesis of biblical orthodoxy.

EXCARNATION IN CULTURE

Excarnation is increasingly a guiding tenet of Western elites. There's nothing Christian about it. The Bible teaches that God's norms are interwoven into the cosmos. These include gravity and thermodynamics. They include economic laws of scarce resources. Moreover, they include his norms for human sexuality. Today's elites don't simply wish to rebel against these laws. They want to circumvent and then abolish them. They have figured out the only way to do this is to bypass reality itself. Their vision of the Good Society is one in which all people are equal in condition, and the "marginalized" are resituated as the apex of culture. If this means redefining reality, so be it.

If the human body as biologically male or female is an impediment to human imagination, sex-"reassignment" surgery is an option. If some humans are smarter, better looking, stronger, or cleverer than others, laws must be imposed that penalize their giftedness and reduce them to the level of their inferiors. Eventually, this means that their gifts must be eliminated to create true equality. If women are naturally superior nurturers and men naturally superior soldiers, men must nurture babies and women must serve in combat. TV and movies must depict lithe 120-pound women as martial arts devotees vanquishing muscular 200-pound male warriors. The ridiculousness of the idea is irrelevant; it's the reality-bending social vision that matters. The body forbids the exercise of the rebellious imagination, so the body must be circumvented and, if necessary, abandoned. Reality doesn't conform to the elite vision of society, so reality is irrelevant.

The excarnation paradigm sees the body simply as a vehicle for the person, the "authentic self." The person, the real you and I, is inside the body, the "ghost in the machine." The body is like an automobile that carts us around. There's a radical disjunction between the authentic, self-aware person, and his body. The body is simply a tool, like a screwdriver or a fork, though a highly complex one.

This anthropology (view of man) has momentous implications. For one thing, it means that if the self is not fully developed, the body is unimportant. This means that there should be no barrier to abortion and euthanasia and mercy killing. After all, it's the self that's important, not the body. If there is no authentic self (or person on the inside), the body is disposable. Remember: the body is only there as a vehicle for the person.[3] This is the grim price we pay as a society for implementing the excarnation vision.

EXCARNATION IN THE CHURCH

The Bible does not exalt spirit over matter; Jesus is Lord of the invisible and visible world (Col. 1:15–17). Yet ever since pagan Greek ideas of the inferiority of the material world infected Christianity, the church has battled with excarnation. Even as the church prays, "Thy will be done on earth as it is in heaven" (Mt. 6:10), many Christians view the world outside the church (economics, politics, entertainment, education, and architecture) as inescapably "carnal" (fleshly) and unfit for Christian influence. So the church retreats to an excarnated spirituality. Prayer, interior dialogue, and contemplation of heaven are considered spiritual, while working to re-criminalize abortion, de-legitimize same-sex "marriage," combat pornography, and reduce government theft programs in the form of confiscatory taxation are relatively unimportant and, in fact, a diversion from the church's real, excarnated tasks. Escape from evil within the created order rather than confrontation with and victory over it is the excarnational agenda. Christianity is reduced to a "personal devotional hobby."[4]

But Advent stares us unflinchingly in the face with the truth that the present world, immaterial and material, is cursed by sin and is to be redeemed by the death and resurrection of our Lord. The most evil being in the universe is pure spirit, but Jesus was born and lived and died and rose from the dead and lives forever in a body. He is profoundly interested in the world, including the material world. He came healing the sick and exorcising demons from tortured bodies. To trust in the Messiah for salvation is to surrender oneself mind, soul, body — our entire self — to him (Rom. 12:1–2).

He is as interested in purging sin from gansta rap and abortion clinics and fraudulent bond-rating agencies and Bauhaus architecture as he is from Christian hearts and families and churches. The cleansing power of the gospel does not simply take souls to heaven; it transforms everything it touches.

CONCLUSION

During this Advent season and at all other times, relish the incarnational life and dismiss the excarnational vision. The body and the material world are not designed for our escape but for joy and victory. Jesus is Lord of all, and a God unashamed to be born into a barn amid farm animals is unashamed to care for and redeem every area of creation and culture presently under the dominion of sin. Advent is a celebration of incarnation that made possible atoning bodily death and victorious bodily resurrection. Our future hope is not excarnation in a false medieval vision of angel babes and halos and harps in heaven but of the new heaven descended to a new earth purged from sin, where God will dwell eternally with us his people — on a profoundly material, but sinless, earth (Rev. 21:1–4).

OUR ROMANTIC MOMENT

Ours is a culture lush in Romanticism, but to grasp it we need to know what it was a reaction against: the European Enlightenment.[1] The Enlightenment began in full force in the 18th century. It was best defined by Immanuel Kant as man's liberation from his self-imposed slavery to external religious authorities like God and the Bible and the church.[2] Man in his reason and experience was now positioned as the measure of all things. But it was *collective* man as the measure. In other words, Enlightenment held up shared human reason and experience as the final authorities. Enlightenment thinkers would talk a great deal about human reason. They meant reason that all people shared. If everybody could just put aside his prejudices and private opinions, we could all arrive at the rational truth. Reason was the same for everybody, if we could just access it and rely on it. We would then agree on religion (a rational but anti-supernatural religion, like Deism), as well as science, education, politics, and the nature of man himself. Man's reason is (or can be) neutral and arrive at the truth without divine revelation.

This rationalism produced a cold, sterile world, and in the late 18th and early 19th centuries, Romanticism emerged as a reaction.[3] Romanticism didn't like the idea of universal or shared reason and experience. It wanted to champion what was *unique* about every individual (or national culture), not what humanity had in common. Romanticism is the first wholesale movement of individualism in world history. The really important thing was individual thinking, feelings, emotions, desires, and interpretations, not what all humans shared. Historians call this "the inward turn"; it's a turning point in Western history. Objective truth outside us is no longer important, whether that truth is God or the Bible or the church or creeds or shared human reason or experience. The most significant thing in life is my inner, subjective life. This is the source of the "cult of authenticity" (see the next chapter).[4]

ROMANTICISM IN EDEN AND THE CHURCH

This is the temptation the serpent offered to Eve in the Garden. "If you eat the forbidden fruit, you'll know good and evil. You will become one of the gods, one of heaven's great court.[5] You'll see the world as only a god can see the world.[6] You'll have a god's-eye view of the universe. You'll have a depth of knowledge that allows you to rise above mere humanity. You are the final arbiter." Today that temptation targets the youthful churched: If you want to engage in premarital sex, that's the new rule. If you decide to date an unbeliever, who's to tell you differently? When you turn 18 years old, you can leave the Faith if you want: who has a right to dictate to you? If you're a young lady and want dress in sexually provocative ways, that's your choice and nobody else's. If you're young man and you lust for pornography, it won't hurt anybody, and nobody else can decide for you. If this church and God stuff seems so unreal, why do you have to bow to it? "I'll live my own life." This is Romanticism in the church. Its roots are in the Garden of Eden.

We've gotten where we are today by gradually shedding all external authorities. When Kant said that Enlightenment is man's coming of age by shedding external authority, he could never have envisioned today's self-autonomy: sexting, juvenile profanity, teenage abortion, "sex-reassignment surgery" (correction: "gender-affirmation surgery"), and other reprehensible practices. But when we throw off authority, particularly God's authority, there's no barrier to anything being permitted.

INHERENT CONFLICT

The Enlightenment idolized humanity in its collective sense: universal human reason and experience. Romanticism and its child postmodernism[7] idolize every individual human in his own uniqueness. The fact that this leads to fatal inner self-contradictions hasn't yet impeded the Romantics. For example, free speech is under attack on our university campuses. Why? Because students believe they have a right not to be offended. Other people must be restrained from saying things that offend me. But what about my speech? Shouldn't I be allowed to express my opinion? If that opinion isn't an acceptable, politically correct opinion, the answer is no, you may not.

The same is true of gay pride parades. These militant gays think they have a right to be homosexual exhibitionists. But what about the right of parents and children who happen to be downtown at the time. Don't they have a right *not* to be exposed to such depravity? And similarly artistic speech. An apostate artist claims the right to depict and display great acts of sexual debauchery or blasphemy, like a crucifix immersed in a jar of urine. Does he have that right of artistic autonomy? If so, do I have the right not to be exposed to it? This is how radical human autonomy leads to inner contradictions. Today's autonomous Romanticism can't account for the inevitable conflict between the expressions of autonomy, or the autonomy or rights of others.

THE CULTURAL CIVIL WAR

For this reason and others, some have predicted that today's culture war will become a civil war.[8] The conflict is basically between the Christian, or-Christian-influenced, vision of culture on the one hand, and the Romantic view of culture on the other. The battle is whether we as a culture will return to God's ways revealed in his word, or charge along the path of worshipping man and his radical individualistic autonomy.

One thing is certain: there can be no compromise between the two.

THE ROMANTIC CULT OF AUTHENTICITY

Before the 19th century, as we just saw, the right kind of life was determined by how you conformed to the Bible or to nature or to reason or experience. But after Romanticism, the best life was the life in which you live out what you're privately believing and feeling. This is the "authentic" life. The "inauthentic" people try to please God or their parents or friends or the wider society's expectations. The authentic people are "true to themselves." They "follow their heart."

IT'S ROUSSEAU'S WORLD, AND WE JUST LIVE IN IT

This complete historical inversion started with the strange but influential French thinker Jean-Jacques Rousseau.[1] Almost everybody before Rousseau believed that human society helps man to be better than he could be as an isolated individual. Human institutions like the family and church and the guild (vocational associations) elevated human existence. Rousseau turned this idea on its head. He believed that we're born into the world innocent, free, and happy, but then human society and culture enslave us, dehumanize us, sadden us. The institutions around us like our parents and friends and church and job conspire to chip away at our true, authentic selves. (By the way, in this sense Marx was deeply Rousseauian.) The goal of life is to rip away these social barriers so that we can be truly authentic.

EXPRESSIVE INDIVIDUALISM

Today we hear this sentiment all the time: "Be true to yourself." "Bernie Sanders is not a regular politician; he's authentic." When rock stars go wild on stage, ripping off their clothes and breaking guitars, we admire them, because they're expressing what they really are. There's even a name for this: "expressive individualism." You validate your unique individualism by expressing yourself, often wildly and bizarrely in public. The idea that it would be better to conform to standards of decency and order (better yet, God's word), would put a crimp on authenticity.

Authenticity has now become a badge of social status. This is especially true with diet. Think only of the great push for eating only food that is organic, local, and sustainable. If you eat this way, incidentally, I'm in no way criticizing you. I'm criticizing the lust for authenticity on the part of people who don't merely eat this way, but want to be known as eating this way. In the words of Andrew Potter, it's a form of "conspicuous authenticity."[2] It's a way of distinguishing themselves from the eating habits of the bourgeois, the unenlightened, the common herd.

For this reason, Rousseau himself was the sworn enemy of social convention. Society was made up of a hierarchy, and he hated that. The lower classes deferred to the upper classes. There was bowing and curtseying. Different classes wore different kinds of clothes. Rousseau abhorred this. For him, people should be judged by the intensity of their conviction and feelings. Social convention demanded that people be courteous, use certain traditional language, stand and talk in certain formal ways. Rousseau considered all of this artificial, totally inauthentic. It's better for people to say exactly what they are feeling on the inside at the time. It's not just that they could be rude, loud, thoughtless, and overbearing. They *should* be this way, as long as that's what they're authentically feeling.

THE LUST FOR SPONTANEITY

This meant, not surprisingly, that romantics prize the spontaneous rather than the planned. If we plan or prepare or premeditate according to certain standards, we're surrendering to external norms. But if we say and do things spontaneously, in the heat of the moment, we're authentic. If we write out our prayers beforehand, we're not being true to ourselves. "Let's be spontaneous!" In every situation, we must "let it all hang out."

Faithfulness, therefore, must take a backseat to spontaneity. Quietly attending the Lord's house week by week and fulfilling your duties to the Lord is boring, formulaic, and inauthentic. The best Christians are those filled with passion, energy, who love to make a public spectacle of their devotion to the Lord.

They're the authentic ones.

LETTERS ON THE CURRENT PROTESTANT REVIVAL OF CLASSICISM, SCHOLASTICISM, AND NATURAL THEOLOGY

⚜

Dr. Sandlin,
Do you know what's driving the resurgence of Classical Apologetics, Neo-platonism, and the subsequent reaction against worldview within Reformed circles?

I'm seeing more and more of this on FB [Facebook] posts, footnotes, books, etc. Otherwise trustworthy and respectable pastors/theologians are pushing this. What's worse, it seems they're promoting it as if the early presup[positional] guys were completely unaware of the Christianizing of Greek categories (as opposed to the Hellenization of Christianity, i.e. Robert Wilken).

As a Kuyperian (generally speaking), it's not that I mind some pushback from these guys — there seems to be some good work being done (i.e., Steven Wedgeworth, The Davenant Institute, etc.) but it seems that they're either (1) lacking self-awareness and hide the fact of their own presuppositions, or (2) prevaricating and purposely misinterpreting the worldview programme. Your thoughts?

Dear ____

These are relevant issues, and I can only speculate about what's driving the revival of classicism, scholasticism, and natural theology.

Like you, I appreciate the work of Davenant and others in stressing a reasonable faith and excavating the "unused past." I suspect at least two dubious factors, however, are at work in this program: one historical, and the other epistemological.

First, the chaos of hypermodernity drives theological and dispositional conservatives into the apparent (but only apparent) safe spaces of the past and to attempts to repristinate it. The historic reality of Christian culture summons Christians amid hypermodernity. The scholastic era was a time when the unity of faith and reason was widely respected, and Christians could conduct scholarship in a generally hospitable climate. The problem is that this faith-reason paradigm ("double-decker" epistemology) compromised the Faith. It did not recognize the inescapably religious character of all thinking, in the lower deck of reason no less than the upper deck of faith. Reason is always captive to the heart, and the heart is inescapably religious. This is what the presuppostionalists from Kuyper onward were wanting to say and it was, after all, just the epistemological implication of good, old-fashioned Reformation theology. Positing reason as a neutral, presupposition-less quality erased or diminished the Bible's depiction of the depravity of the "natural" mind. Roman Catholic historian Christopher Dawson observed that when Enlightenment needed a paradigm for the super-exaltation of reason, it had one ready at hand: the scholastic nature-grace (faith) distinction.[1] It simply lopped off the upper deck of faith-grace. For this reason, I agree with Brian Mattson's hint that if the current advocates of natural theology were to succeed, they would return us to a way of thinking that helped give us the very secularism that afflicts us.[2]

Second, I think these folks are under the impression that the epistemology of worldview thinkers and presuppositionalists too closely resembles philosophical idealism and Kantian epistemology (this is not a new charge, by the way). In our postmodern times that privilege constructivist epistemologies and are attempting to reinvent reality via moves like transgenderism, those suspicions might seem well founded. By "constructivist epistemologies," I mean views of knowledge that see nature as a mass of chaotic stuff that the mind must order and reorder in order to supply meaning. In today's climate, it means also that man creates his own reality: nature (if there even is such a thing) is the clay, and we are the creators. To be sure, we worldview thinkers deny the possibility of unaided reason and the neutrality of the knower. Yet we're emphatically opposed to constructivist epistemologies. We hold to a meaning-laden creation with the greatest force. Creation is foundational, and the gospel is a tributary (though a vital one, to be sure) in the massive Christian worldview river. Anybody who has read Herman Dooyeweerd knows that his theory of law spheres ("creational norms") rejects any epistemology that denies the world brims over with divinely inscribed meaning. He and we only want to point out that man never encounters creation in a neutral way: the heart (the spiritual organ) is never inert. It worships either the Creator or the creation. No one ever accused Herman Bavinck of a diminished view of creation. John M. Frame, the leading presuppositionalist of our time, just write a book on creation. It is possible (no, essential) to embrace the highest view of a meaning-laded creation and simultaneously the clearest understanding of reason as non-neutral, and captive to the heart.

The early presuppositionalists were certainly as aware as liberals like Harnack of the Hellenization of subapostolic Christianity. Indeed, Dooyeweerd made this a cornerstone of his epistemology and social theory, and Van Til made it a cornerstone of his apologetics. The liberal answer was to read this Hellenization back in the New Testament. The presuppositionalist answer was to adopt the Hebraic-biblical paradigm as a corrective to the Hellenization.

I hope this helps. I'm eager to see you and your son at the Runner Academy this July. We'll be highlighting all these distinctions and more, and laying out an extensive Reformational worldview.

COVENANT VERSUS AUTONOMY

Ours is an age of autonomy ("self-law"). Of course, autonomy has been around since the Fall. What's different today, as we noted earlier, is that the secular West has created sophisticated rationales for it. It's not just that man is autonomous; it's that man *should* be autonomous, and any other way is unnatural and enslaving. Man hasn't simply broken free from God's law; he's now trying to break free from creation itself.

Transgenderism is one such attempt to vanquish God's created order. Man's imagination mustn't be subject to any constraints. Man has a right to be anything he wants to be, and if anybody gets in the way, that impediment must be legally removed. Male athletes that see themselves as transgendered must be given the right to participate in women's sports contests. It doesn't matter that this move disadvantages women: contra-creational rights trump women's rights.

This autonomy has moved into the church. More churches and ministries are capitulating to so-called same-sex "marriage" and "-attraction." This includes ministers and churches in such allegedly conservative groups as the Southern Baptist Convention and the Presbyterian Church in America. The fact that these views and acts are flatly anti-biblical seems not to matter. What's most important is conforming to what Francis Schaeffer called "forms of the world spirit." The driving force in Western culture today, postmodernism, unleashed radical autonomy, especially sexual autonomy. It must tower over all else in culture, even in the church.

This is an attack on the very roots of the covenant: that God is the suzerain and we are the vassals. Jesus is Lord, and we are his subjects. This isn't a decision we make only at conversion. We must make it again every day: will we surrender our will and desires to our King, the one who bought us with his own blood? The great Swiss reformer Heinrich Bullinger (Zwingli's successor) was correct, therefore, when he declared that

> [T]he entire sum of piety consists in these very brief main points of the covenant. Indeed, it is evident that nothing else was handed down to the saints of all ages, throughout the entire Scripture, other than what is included in these main points of the covenant.... Compare, if you will, the law, the prophets, and the very epistles of the apostles with these main points of the covenant, and you will discover that all of them return to this center as if to a target.[1]

But we aren't only oath-bound to God; he's oath-bound to us. He promises he'll never leave us or forsake us. Nothing can separate us from the love of God in Jesus Christ our Lord (Rom. 8:35f.). And by nothing, I mean nothing. He promises to answer our earnest prayers,[2] meet our greatest needs, give us the strength to defeat the world, the flesh and the Devil. We don't bow to a weak, ineffectual suzerain (an ancient great lord). He's King of kings and Lord of lords. He rules from the heavens and rides on the clouds and accomplishes his will in the earth. No one can thwart his purposes.

If today you feel overwhelmed, weak, impoverished, rudderless, know this: you have a great suzerain, a great King, who is covenantally bound to you. It's not simply that he might help or might not. He's willingly tethered himself to you by covenant. He can't do otherwise. Some things God cannot do, not because he is not all-powerful, but because he has willingly bound himself to his promises. One of those promises is to be perseveringly faithful to you and me as his covenant people. Hold him to his covenant promises. He delights when we remind him of his promises to us, because that shows that we take his word seriously (Is. 45:11; 62:6–7). Take God at his covenant word.

SACCHARINE PIETY

Religiosity is not religion, and piety untethered to the Bible, wafting to the heavens for both God and man to admire, is not true piety. It is saccharine piety, a sickly sweet religiosity that impresses the sentimentally superficial but earns the scorn of the godly and, more significantly, of God himself. It is a mark of the sinful human condition, but in large scale it was imported into Western Christianity with the medieval Sacred Heart of Jesus and later with Revivalism (crisis experience is the chief criterion of true religion) and Romanticism (feelings and emotions and subjective experience trump all else). Saccharine piety now pervades even the most conservative sectors of Christianity.

THE PIOUSLY SACCHARINE JESUS VERSUS INFERIOR OLD TESTAMENT LAW

Atlanta megachurch pastor Andy Stanley writes that Jesus Christ came to offer a new and higher ethic, replacing God's revelatory moral law of the Old Testament: "We need to stop mixing the old with the new, because God has given us something better in Jesus Christ and his new command."[1] This is classic antinomianism (lawlessness).

There's no other or better name for it. The fact that Jesus' blood-shedding inaugurated the new covenant in no way invalidates the moral law, whose insertion into the hearts of Christians is one of the chief benefits the new covenant was instituted to impart (Heb. 8:7–12). Stanley may personally live a godly, exemplary life, and I am sure he does, but his teaching is contra-biblical and is leading thousands of Christians astray. Jesus Christ does not lead his people to a "higher" (or "deeper") morality than the moral law of God found in both Old and New Testaments, and following this antinomian teaching is not true piety but merely saccharine disobedience.

PIOUSLY SACCHARINE PRAYERS

Danish existential Christian philosopher Søren Kierkegaard declares that giving thanks to God is superior to petitionary prayer.[2] This is a common assumption, despite the fact that the Bible says nothing of the kind. How pervasive is the saccharine piety that to ask God to provide blessings for his people is at best second-level spirituality, inferior to worshiping or thanking God, and at worst positively "carnal" and self-centered. In radical contrast, Jesus promises his disciples (and by extension, us), "[W]hatever you ask in My name, that I will do, that the Father may be glorified in the Son. If you ask anything in My name, I will do it" (Jn. 14:13–14). To ask the Father in the Son's name is to glorify the Son. To refuse to ask under the guise of saccharine piety is to deny glory to the Son, whom the Father delights to honor in answering his people's prayer.

MORE SPIRITUAL THAN THE BIBLE

In the 90s I wrote a review of Jim West's delightful *Drinking with Calvin and Luther!*,[3] which details the Protestant reformers' drinking preferences. I pointed out in my review that while the Bible strictly forbids drunkenness, it by no means prohibits the moderate consumption of alcohol. I had a dissenting letter from a lady asserting that while it's true the Bible doesn't forbid drinking alcoholic beverages, God "holds his people to a higher standard," i.e., than the Bible. But there is no higher standard of righteousness than the Bible, which is a partial description of God's holiness.

PEACE THAT GOD DOESN'T GIVE

I once counseled a young married woman trying to convince me to endorse her divorce from her husband, despite the fact that, though sinful, he'd done nothing to violate his marital vows. Finally, in exasperation, she declared, "Well, I've prayed, and God has given me peace in my heart about it."

I replied, "You might have peace in your heart, but God didn't give it. God never granted internal peace to one person to do one thing contrary to his written will." In this case, as in others, the "inner light" of saccharine piety is a quick way to the outer darkness.

PIOUSLY ROBBING THE PASTOR

I have known churches served by faithful, sacrificial pastors who must work outside the church to support their family, while the church had the resources to support him yet were enamored of supporting foreign missionaries or other outside ministries, or erecting a new sanctuary. They lean on their saccharine piety to obscure their disobedience. In radical contrast, the Bible demands that faithful ministers be compensated double for their labors, that is, twice what would normally be paid to a worker (1 Tim. 5:17). But this requirement would likely not be sufficiently "spiritual" to the saccharine pietists, for whom the trappings of religiosity trump obedience to God's word.

THE EVIL OF "UNCONDITIONAL FORGIVENESS"

One of the great mantras of modern evangelicalism is "unconditional forgiveness." It is thought a sacrificial act of piety to forgive those who have wronged us, even if they've not repented. This is not piety, but disobedience, making a mockery of the Cross. As Ardel Caneday has written, since we're commanded to forgive in the manner in which God forgives, and if he demands repentance as a condition of forgiveness and we do not, we have wrongly forgiven.[4] We create the impression that God does not demand repentance. God demands repentance, but we are apparently more pious than God. This tack is lawlessness under the guise of grace. Yet the one who insists on biblical standards of forgiveness is often deemed heartless by the denizens of saccharine piety. They are the heartless ones, considering the cross so trivial as to reduce its standards to conform to sinful man's comfort.

THE PIOUS LEGALISTS

Often saccharine piety, like that of the old Pharisaic party, abandons God's law in order to install its own, new standard of piety. Jesus states: "For laying aside the commandment of God, you hold the tradition of men . . . . All too well you reject the commandment of God, that you may keep your tradition (Mk. 7:8–9). Emergent evangelical pastor Doug Pagitt is scandalized that so many evangelicals have made the pro-life cause a cornerstone of their political agenda:

> These conservative leaders [supporting Trump and the Republican Party] are willing, at all costs, to make a moral trade — anti-abortion laws and court decisions in exchange for basic human dignity.... pursuit of the common good means taking time to stand with women, people of color, immigrants, refugees, the poor and the sick.[5]

By "standing with women," the article refers to the call to attack the judicially innocent preborn and the unjustly pilloried Brett Kavanaugh. By "people of color, immigrants, refugees" he means an immigration policy that subverts the rule of law and imports multiculturalism. By "stand[ing] with the poor and sick," he denotes socialism and nationalized health care. What he does advocate violates God's moral law, or is not addressed by it. What he marginalizes (the life of preborn children) divine law treasures and protects. Pagitt substitutes saccharine, heart-string-tugging piety for God's holy, life-giving law.

CONCLUSION

We read in 1 Samuel 15 of God's command that Israel's first king, Saul, annihilate the Amalekites and their prized possessions for that nation's vicious treatment of his people. Saul instead preserved their king as well as the best of the possessions as war booty. When Samuel the prophet rebuked him for his flagrant disobedience, Saul, good saccharine pietist that he was, replied that "the people" confiscated the best of the animals for the purpose to sacrificing to the Lord. Samuel's reply should ring forever in the ears of all other saccharine pietists (vv. 22–23):

> "Has the Lord as great delight in burnt offerings and sacrifices, [a]s in obeying the voice of the Lord? Behold, to obey is better than sacrifice, [a]nd to heed than the fat of rams.
> For rebellion is as the sin of witchcraft, [a]nd stubbornness is as iniquity and idolatry. Because you have rejected the word of the Lord, He also has rejected you ...."

NOTES

1. THE CHRISTIAN ASSAULT ON CHRISTENDOM

1. Oscar Cullmann, *The Earliest Christian Confessions* (London: Lutterworth Press, 1949), 23.
2. Jasper Adams, "The Relation of Christianity to Civil Government in the United States," in *Religion and Politics in the Early Republic*, Daniel L. Dreisbach, ed. (Lexington, Kentucky: University of Kentucky Press, 1996), 39–58.
3. Christopher Dawson, *The Historic Reality of Christian Culture* (London: Routledge and Kegan Paul, 1960).
4. Peter Gay, *The Age of Enlightenment* (New York: Time-Life, 1966).
5. For a sympathetic treatment of a principal recent, and the most pervasive external, enemy of Christendom, marinated in both Enlightenment and Romanticism, see Peter Gay, *Modernism: The Lure of Heresy* (New York and London: W. W. Norton, 2008).
6. Brian D. McLaren, "Church Emerging: Or Why I Still Use the Word Postmodern but with Mixed Feelings," in *An Emergent Manifesto of Hope*, Doug Pagitt and Tony Jones, eds. (Grand Rapids: Baker, 2007), 148.
7. Ibid., 151.
8. David VanDrunen, "Calvin, Kuyper and 'Christian Culture,'" in *Always Reformed: Essays in Honor of W. Robert Godfrey*, R. Scott Clark and Joel E. Kim, eds. (Escondido, California: Westminster Seminary California, 2010) 135–153.
9. Ibid., 149–152.
10. 140.
11. Ibid., 141–153.
12. Richard J. Mouw, *Abraham Kuyper: A Short and Personal Introduction* (Grand rapids: Eerdmans, 2011).
13. Ibid., 151.
14. Alvin J. Schmidt, *Under the Influence, How Christianity Transformed Civilization* (Grand Rapids: Zondervan, 2001).

2. FIRST, THE KINGDOM

1. R. T. France, "Kingdom of God," *Dictionary for Theological Interpretation of the Bible*, Kevin J. Vanhoozer, ed. (Grand Rapids: Baker, 2005), 420.
2. Karl Barth, *God in Action* (Manhasset, New York: Round Table Press, 1963), 49.
3. Joseph Boot, *For Mission, The Need for Scriptural Cultural Theology* (Grimsby, Ontario: EICC Publications, 2018), 8–29.
4. John Calvin, *Institutes of the Christian Religion*, trans. Henry Beveridge (Peabody, Massachusetts: Hendrickson, 2008), Bk. 4, Ch. 20, Sec. 4.

NOTES

3. STAND YOUR GROUND IN THE EVIL DAY

1. Francis A. Schaeffer, *The Great Evangelical Disaster* (Westchester, Illinois: Crossway, 1984), 111–140.
2. Of course, justice (= righteousness) should be social, and a culture must be just, according to God's moral law, but this is not what most "Social Justice Warriors" mean at all. They are simply Leftists with a pious veneer.
3. Dan Hannan, "The Continuing Creep of Social Injustice," *Washington Examiner*, February 12, 2019, 56
4. Francis A. Schaeffer, *The Great Evangelical Disaster*, 99.
5. John E. Ashbrook, *Axioms of Separation* (Mentor, Ohio: Here I Stand Books, n.d.), 4–9.
6. John Calvin, *Commentary on the Epistle of Paul to the Ephesians* in *Calvin's Commentaries* (Grand Rapids: Baker, 1993), 21:310–311.

4. RESISTANCE THEOLOGY VERSUS RESIGNATION THEOLOGY

1. Ralph D. Winter, "The Mission of the Kingdom," in *Perspectives on the World Christian Movement*, Ralph D. Winter and Steven C. Hawthorne, eds. (Pasadena, California: William Carey Library, 2009, 4th edition), 573.
2. P. Andrew Sandlin, *Crush the Evil, God's Promises Heal Man's Pessimism* (Coulterville, California: Center for Cultural Leadership, 2016).
3. David Scott Clark, *The Message from Patmos* (London, Forgotten Books, 2018, n.d.).
4. David Wells, "Prayer: Rebelling Against the Status Quo," in *Perspectives on the World Christian Movement*, 160.
5. Colin E. Gunton, *The Triune Creator* (Grand Rapids: Eerdmans, 1998), 16.

5. A CURSE ON ABORTICIDE

1. John E. Ashbrook, "Aborticide!" *The Projector*, May, 1979, 1, 3–4, 9.
2. Mary Eberstadt, *Adam and Eve After the Pill* (San Francisco: Ignatius Press, 2012), 14.
3. Kemper Krabb, "A Malediction," https://desiderantangeli.blogspot.com/2009/01/malediction.html, accessed November 17, 2019.

6. BIBLICAL SEXUALITY, SIMPLY EXPLAINED

1. A. W. Tozer, *A Treasury of A. W. Tozer* (Grand Rapids: Baker, 1980), 210–219.

8. REFORMING ONLY THE FAMILY AND CHURCH WON'T SUFFICE

1. Francis A. Schaeffer, *The Complete Works of Francis A. Schaeffer* (Westchester, Illinois: Crossway, 1982), 5:423.
2. Roger Scruton, *Fools, Frauds, and Firebrands: Thinkers of the New Left* (London and New York: Bloomsbury, 2015), 2015.

9. LIBERAL CHRISTIANITY ISN'T

1. J. Gresham Machen, *Christianity and Liberalism* (Grand Rapids: Eerdmans, 1923).
2. John Jefferson Davis, "Kant and the Problem of Religious Knowledge," in *Perspectives on Evangelical Theology*, Kenneth S. Kantzer and Stanley N. Gundry, eds. (Grand Rapids: Baker, 1979), 231–250.

10. ARMED TO THE TEETH, PACIFIST TO THE CORE

1. Herman Dooyeweerd, *Roots of Western Culture* (Ancaster, Ontario, Canada: Paideia Press, 2012), 28–36.
2. Roderick Campbell, *Israel and the New Covenant* (Philadelphia: Presbyterian and Reformed, 1954), 306.
3. J. Marcellus Kik, *An Eschatology of Victory* (Phillipsburg, New Jersey: Presbyterian and Reformed, 1971).
4. Thomas Sowell, *Intellectuals and Society* (New York: basic Books, 2009), 215–225.

11. CREATION: THE EVANGELICAL FAILURE

1. D. W. Bebbington, *Evangelicalism in Modern Britain* (London and New York: Routledge, 1989), 2–17.
2. Colin E. Gunton, *Christ and Creation* (Eugene, Oregon: Wipf and Stock, 1992, 2005).

12. THE REVENGE OF THE COSMOS

1. Anthony Bradley, "A Conflict of Christian Visions: Gen. 1-2 vs. Gen. 3 Christianity," http://blog.acton.org/archives/58497-a-conflict-of-christian-visions-gen-1-2-vs-gen-3-christianity.html, accessed December 8, 2015.
2. Walter Truett Anderson, *Reality Isn't What it Used to Be* (New York: HarperCollins, 1990).

13. THE THINNESS OF THE CHURCH

1. I borrowed this language from my friend and colleague Brian Mattson. He employed it at the inaugural Evan Runner Academy 2019 to describe art as thin or thick, chiding much modern Christian art as thin. I later counseled a friend about his vexing church situation, and adapted the thinness metaphor to assist him.
2. S. U. Zuidema, *Communication and Confrontation* (Toronto: Wedge Publishing, 1972), 36–51.
3. The church must exude compassion, but it is never compassionate to excuse sin. This is a lack of compassion.

14. THE PROGRESSIVES' MARCH TOWARD GOD'S JUDGMENT

1. Kenneth Minogue, *Alien Powers, The Pure Theory of Ideology* (New York: St. Martin's, 1985), 13.
2. John Baillie, *The Belief in Progress* (New York: Charles Scribner's, 1951), 42–87.
3. Isaiah Berlin, *The Power of Ideas* (Princeton and Oxford: Princeton University Press, 2000), 115–125.
4. Peter Gay, *Modernism, The Lure of Heresy* (New York and London: W.W. Norton, 2008), 3–4.
5. Thomas C. Oden, "Can Anything Good Come Out of Liberalism? One Pilgrim's Regress," in *Pilgrims on the Sawdust Trail*, Timothy George, ed. (Grand Rapids: Baker, 2004), 160.
6. Thomas Molnar, *Utopia, The Perennial Heresy* (New York: Sheed & Ward, 1967).

15. A NOTE ON FAITH, WORKS, AND JUSTIFICATION

1. A more recent and superb articulation can be found in John Murray, "Justification," in *Collected Writings of John Murray* (Carlisle, Pennsylvania: Banner of Truth, 1977), 2:202–222.

16. CHRISTMAS VERSUS EXCARNATION

1. Charles Taylor, *A Secular Age* (Cambridge, Massachusetts and London, England: Belknap, 2007), 288.
2. Benjamin Walker, *Gnosticism, Its History and influence* (Wellingborough, Northamptonshire, England: Aquarian Press, 1983, 1989).
3. Robert P. George, "Gnostic Liberalism," *First Things*, December 2016, 33–38.
4. Stephen C. Perks, *The Great Decommission* (Taunton, England: Kuyper Foundation, 2011), 20.

17. OUR ROMANTIC MOMENT

1. Peter Gay, *The Age of Enlightenment* (New York: Time-Life, 1966).
2. Immanuel Kant, "What Is Enlightenment?" http://www.columbia.edu/acis/ets/CCREAD/etscc/kant.html, accessed July 6, 2018.
3. Isaiah Berlin, *The Roots of Romanticism* (Princeton, New Jersey: Princeton University Press, 1999).
4. Charles Guignon, *Being Authentic* (London and New York: Routledge, 2004), 49–77.
5. Bruce K. Waltke, *Genesis, A Commentary* (Grand Rapids: Zondervan, 2001), 91.
6. Robert S. Candlish, *Commentary on Genesis* (Grand Rapids: Zondervan, 1866 reprint), 1:64–65.
7. For a genealogy and description of postmodernism, see David Harvey, *The Condition of Postmodernity* (Malden, Massachusetts: Blackwell, 1995), 3–65.
8. Angelo M. Codevilla, "The Cold Civil War," *Claremont Review of Books*, Vol. XVII, No. 2 [Spring 2017], 24–27.

18. THE ROMANTIC CULT OF AUTHENTICITY

1. Isaiah Berlin, *Freedom and Its Betrayal* (Princeton and Oxford: Princeton University Press, 2002), 27–49.
2. Andrew Potter, *The Authenticity Hoax* (New York: HarperCollins, 2010), 103–135.

19. LETTERS ON THE CURRENT PROTESTANT REVIVAL OF CLASSICISM, SCHOLASTICISM, AND NATURAL THEOLOGY

1. Christopher Dawson, "Rationalism and Intellectualism: The Religious Elements in the Rationalist Tradition," *Enquiries into Religion and Its Culture* (London and New York: Sheed & Ward, 1933), 146–148.
2. Brian G. Mattson, "Doubting Thomas (Aquinas)," http://drbrianmattson.com/journal/2016/6/8/doubting-thomas, accessed October 30, 2019.

20. COVENANT VERSUS AUTONOMY

1. Heinrich Bullinger, *A Brief Exposition of the One Eternal Testament or Covenant of God*, in *Fountainhead of Federalism*, Charles S. McCoy and Wayne Baker, eds. (Louisville, Kentucky: Westminster/John Knox Press, 1991), 112–113.
2. P. Andrew Sandlin, *Prayer Changes Things, Curing Timid Piety* (Coulterville, California, 2018).

21. SACCHARINE PIETY

1. Andy Stanley, "Jesus Ended the Old Covenant Once and for All," https://www.christianitytoday.com/ct/2018/october-web-only/andy-stanley-irresistible-response-to-foster.html, accessed September 13, 2019.
2. Søren Kierkegaard, *Spiritual Writings*, *George* Pattison, trans. (New York: HarperPerennial, 2010), 7–9.
3. (Lincoln, California: Oakdown, 2003).
4. Ardel Caneday, *Must Christians Always Forgive?* (Mount Hermon, California: Center for Cultural Leadership, 2011).
5. Doug Pagitt, "Evangelicals Are Paying High Moral Price for Anti-Abortion Gains. What Would Jesus Do?" https://www.usatoday.com/story/opinion/2018/10/21/donald-trump-abortion-cost-evangelicals-moral-high-ground-column/1686348002/, accessed September 13, 2019.

ABOUT THE AUTHOR

P. Andrew Sandlin is Founder and President of the Center for Cultural Leadership. A cultural theologian, he is faculty at the Blackstone Legal Fellowship, Edinburgh Theological Seminary, the H. Evan Runner International Academy of Cultural Leadership, and the Worldview Leadership League. He and his wife Sharon have five adult children and three grandchildren.

ABOUT THE CENTER FOR CULTURAL LEADERSHIP

The Center for Cultural Leadership believes that culture should be Christian — not by political coercion, but by spiritual conversion. Christian is what Western culture was for 1000 years, and this what it should be today. This means that Christians should lead the culture — as fathers, mothers, college students, businessmen, attorneys, pastors, educators, software writers, salesmen, technicians, politicians, physicians, clerks, and so forth.

But CCL does not just believe Christians should lead. It shows them how to lead.

CCL is not only training Christian activists. Lots of people are doing that, and some are doing well. We're educating and equipping Christian transformationists. It's not enough to be active; you actually have to transform things.

This is what we're after.